COMPUTING
FROM THE ABACUS TO THE iPAD

COMPUTING AND CONNECTING IN THE 21ST CENTURY

COMPUTING
FROM THE ABACUS TO THE iPAD

EDITED BY ROBERT CURLEY, MANAGER, SCIENCE AND TECHNOLOGY

Britannica
Educational Publishing

IN ASSOCIATION WITH

ROSEN
EDUCATIONAL SERVICES

Published in 2012 by Britannica Educational Publishing
(a trademark of Encyclopædia Britannica, Inc.)
in association with Rosen Educational Services, LLC
29 East 21st Street, New York, NY 10010.

Copyright © 2012 Encyclopædia Britannica, Inc. Britannica, Encyclopædia Britannica, and the Thistle logo are registered trademarks of Encyclopædia Britannica, Inc. All rights reserved.

Rosen Educational Services materials copyright © 2012 Rosen Educational Services, LLC. All rights reserved.

Distributed exclusively by Rosen Educational Services.
For a listing of additional Britannica Educational Publishing titles, call toll free (800) 237-9932.

First Edition

Britannica Educational Publishing
Michael I. Levy: Executive Editor
J.E. Luebering: Senior Manager
Marilyn L. Barton: Senior Coordinator, Production Control
Steven Bosco: Director, Editorial Technologies
Lisa S. Braucher: Senior Producer and Data Editor
Yvette Charboneau: Senior Copy Editor
Kathy Nakamura: Manager, Media Acquisition
Robert Curley : Manager, Science and Technology

Rosen Educational Services
Alexandra Hanson-Harding: Editor
Nelson Sá: Art Director
Cindy Reiman: Photography Manager
Matthew Cauli: Designer, Cover Design
Introduction by Heather Miller

Library of Congress Cataloging-in-Publication Data

Computing : from the abacus to the iPad / edited by Robert Curley.
    p. cm.—(Computing and connecting in the 21st century)
"In association with Britannica Educational Publishing, Rosen Educational Services."
Includes bibliographical references and index.
ISBN 978-1-61530-660-2 (library binding)
1. Electronic data processing—Juvenile literature. 2. Computers—Juvenile literature. I. Curley, Robert, 1955-
QA76.23.C665 2012
004—dc23

                                                                      2011016185

Manufactured in the United States of America

Cover (abacus) Shutterstock.com; cover (iPad) Justin Sullivan/Getty Images; p. iii © www.istockphoto.com/Rick Lord; pp. v, vi, vii, viii, xi (background graphic) © www.istockphoto.com/Simfo; pp. 1, 20, 41, 66, 95, 134, 137, 140 Ian Waldie/Getty Images; pp. 4, 5, 15, 16, 25, 57, 58, 83, 84, 115, 129, 130 © www.istockphoto.com/Andrey Volodin; pp. 64, 82, 91, 99 © www.istockphoto.com/Karl Dolenc; remaining interior background image © www.istockphoto.com/Johan Ramberg

On pages x-xi: People wait to register to vote as an official records data on a laptop in Lagos, Nigeria, on Jan. 15, 2011. Making elections fairer is just one of many uses of computers. *Pius Utomi Ekpei/AFP/Getty Images*

CONTENTS

INTRODUCTION

Perhaps few inventions have changed the course of human history as much as the computer. It has literally changed the way that most of us live. Today, we can be anywhere in the world and, with a few taps of our fingertips on a keyboard, we can join a chat room whose members live on different continents. We can earn college degrees online while living in remotest Alaska or the Australian Outback. We can find the fastest route to drive across town or across the country. We can discover information about our ancestors by accessing digitized shipping and census records. And thanks to computers, millions are now able to work from home, balancing their family responsibilities with the demands of their jobs. Most of these capabilities would have been unthinkable even just 20 years ago.

So how did we come so far so fast with computers and information technology? This book provides an overview of the history of computer development. As you read, you'll meet some of the remarkable personalities and intriguing technology that contributed to the digital age that we are now living in.

To find the first tool that even slightly resembled a computer, many would travel all the way back to 500 BCE and point to the abacus. An abacus was used for counting and for performing the adding, subtracting, multiplying, and dividing functions common in business at the time- This device was the first in human history that helped humans manage and store numbers.

The first instance of programming occurred early in the Industrial Revolution, in the textile trade. Joseph-Marie Jacquard invented a loom in 1804-5 that used a punch card method of passing instructions to the machine. Each punch card had holes in particular spots. These holes told the mechanical loom which threads to weave in which pattern. In this way, once the loom had been programmed with a set of punched cards, it could act intelligently and weave a wide range of patterns and designs without human assistance.

While Jacquard's loom involved no mathematical processing, his ingenious punch cards were used again and again in later stages of the development of the computer.

In the 1820s, Cambridge University–educated mathematician Charles Babbage designed a calculating machine called the Difference Engine. In Babbage's day, mariners had to consult logarithm tables in order to make correct calculations for navigation. One major problem was that the logarithm tables contained a fair number of errors. Babbage's aim was to mechanize the process for producing logarithm tables so that no error would be produced at all. Babbage's Difference Engine was a brilliant prototype whose sophisticated design inspired centuries of computer programmers. However, before he had fully executed the Difference Engine, Babbage was on to his next and even more ambitious invention: the Analytical Engine.

The Analytical Engine was the predecessor of the modern-day computer. Babbage designed it so that a number of programs could run on it. It took its inspiration from Jacquard's loom. In much the same way that different punch cards could change the weaving patterns performed by Jacquard's loom, so could punch cards enter mathematical data and decide the specific calculations to run on the analytical engine. In fact, Augusta Ada King, the Countess of Lovelace, a mathematician (and daughter of Lord Byron), wrote, "The analytical engine weaves algebraic patterns just as the Jacquard loom weaves flowers and leaves." Sadly, Babbage lacked the funds to completely build the analytical engine. Still, although his work on both engines never progressed beyond the prototype stage, his avant-garde approach to information processing made him the undisputed father of the modern computer.

The next major advancement in the development of information processing came as a result of the 1890 census in the United States. U.S. law mandates that a census of the entire nation be taken every decade. Up until the 1890s, this massive process was done by individuals with very little machine assistance. Not surprisingly, it typically took years to produce the census each time.

Hoping to spur innovation, the government launched a contest to find the best method of collecting and reporting data for the census. A young mathematician named Herman Hollerith won. A former employee in the Census Office, Hollerith understood the vast clerical enterprise involved in census-taking and had definite ideas about how to mechanize the work of clerks. He designed an elaborate and highly integrated system to tabulate the census data. At the heart of Hollerith's systems were punch cards whose functionality was similar to those on Jacquard's loom. Data about individuals was collected on punch cards. Hollerith's design called for machines that could quickly tabulate the punch cards.

Hollerith's tabulating machine was a huge success. It saved the government millions of dollars and delivered the data swiftly. Hollerith was able to commercialize his invention. Soon nations all over the world, including Czarist Russia and the United Kingdom, paid vast sums for Hollerith's system. Railroads also used Hollerith's system for managing their business. In 1896, Hollerith formed the Tabulating Machine Company, which eventually grew into what would become IBM.

While practical applications of information technology were demanded by government and business, the theoretical foundations of this new science were established at universities. In particular, Harvard, MIT, and Cambridge University in England contributed substantially to the development of computers in the early 20th century. A notable example is Vannevar Bush, an engineer at MIT who in 1930 designed and produced the Differential Analyzer, the first modern analog computer. The Differential Analyzer was able to solve certain types of differential equations that were critical to the work of physicists and engineers. These equations were tedious and time consuming to solve. By doing this work, the Differential Analyzer sped up the process of research and development.

Between the years 1939 and 1944, Harvard professor Howard Aiken made a remarkable contribution to computing with the Harvard Mark I. Produced in collaboration with IBM, the Harvard Mark I was the first fully automated large-scale calculators.

World War II spurred the next major step forward in computing.

John Mauchly and J. Presper Eckert responded to

the challenge with the development of the Electronic Numerical Integrator and Computer. Also known as ENIAC, this machine was the first programmable general-purpose electronic computer. It relied on vacuum tubes to run at electronic speeds and could perform calculations far faster than previous electromechanical machines.

Throughout most of the 20th century, computers were used mainly by a small group of engineers, academics, and other scientists. It was not until the late 1970s and 1980s that the personal computer revolution began. What spurred the development of these small computers was a group of enthusiastic amateurs, many of them living in what later became known as California's Silicon Valley. The first such computer came in a kit and was called the Altair.

But it was Bill Gates that enabled the personal computer revolution to change the way people work and communicate. In 1974, Gates and his Harvard classmate Paul Allen were math and computer science students who set their sights on making it big in the burgeoning computer industry. They wrote a version of the BASIC computer program, which had been invented in the 1960s for the Altair. In an act of brilliant business acumen, Gates and Allen never sold their program. Instead, they licensed it. This allowed them to retain the rights over their version of BASIC and later license a more sophisticated version of it to IBM, the largest computer company in the world. Gates and Allen called their company Microsoft. Microsoft created versions of BASIC for almost every new type of computer. By his early 30s, Gates was the country's youngest billionaire.

The genius of Microsoft's BASIC program (and later, its MS-DOS program, and still later, its Windows program) is that it made the personal computer extremely valuable for the everyday demands of office workers. Information processing, whether it was creating a budget on a spreadsheet, editing a document, or making a presentation, was far easier than it had ever been before. The storage and retrieval of documents was now a simple process that no longer required huge amounts of space. It could all be saved on a microchip in a computer.

Steve Jobs and Steve Wozniak , the founders of Apple, made the first truly successful commercial foray into the personal computer market with their Apple, Lisa, and Macintosh computers. Apple products from the beginning married computing innovation with a keen design sensibility and ease of use that endeared them to the graphics design and publishing professionals who would become their core market.

Since the personal computer revolution of the 1980s, there has been enormous innovation in the computer industry. Apple in particular has been responsible for some of the most revolutionary inventions, including the iPhone and, more recently, the iPad. Both inventions have made a major impact on the communications, music, business, and publishing industries.

The future of computing is in the hands of the bright women and men who commit themselves to the field of computer science. If the young computer scientists of today are anything like the geniuses Babbage, Hollerith, and Gates, the next century should bring the world some remarkable advancements in computers and the way we live.

CHAPTER 1

EARLY HISTORY

A computer might be described with deceptive simplicity as "an apparatus that performs routine calculations automatically." Such a definition would be deceptive because it would be based on a naive and narrow view of calculation as a strictly mathematical process. In reality, calculation underlies many activities that are not normally thought of as mathematical. Walking across a room, for instance, is a complex problem that requires many calculations, most of them subconscious and hardly mathematical. In order for a machine to be considered a true computer, it would have to prove itself capable of solving a similarly vast array of problems—for instance, balancing a bank account or even (in the case of a guidance system for robots) walking across a room.

For the true power of computing to be realized, therefore, the naive view of calculation has to be overcome. However, before this milestone was passed in human history, inventors laboured long to produce devices that would relieve them of the repetitive work of manipulating numbers and doing the same mathematical calculations over and over again. Most of the devices that they invented—ranging from the rod-and-bead abacus to the slide rule to the desktop adding machine—were not computers, but collectively they made a necessary step in that direction. One great exception was the programmable machines conceived in the 19th century by Englishman Charles Babbage. These contained the elements of a true computer, but even in their case the technology of Babbage's day prevented his designs from being realized.

COMPUTER PRECURSORS

Computer precursors were devices that performed simple mathematical calculations or directed the movements of machine parts. Though not computers in the modern sense, they established the practice of executing such functions mechanically.

THE ABACUS

The earliest known calculating device is probably the abacus. It dates back at least to 1100 BCE and is still in use today, particularly in Asia. Now, as then, it typically consists of a rectangular frame with thin parallel rods strung with beads. Long before any systematic positional notation was

A girl practices on an abacus during the 27th annual abacus contest on May 20, 2009, in Tokyo, Japan. American schools in Japan use abacuses to develop children's calculating ability. Junko Kimura/Getty Images.

adopted for the writing of numbers, the abacus assigned different units, or weights, to each rod—i.e., ones, tens, hundreds, and so on. This scheme allowed a wide range of numbers to be represented by just a few beads and, together with the invention of zero in India, may have inspired the invention of the Hindu-Arabic number system. In any case, abacus beads can be readily manipulated to perform the common arithmetical operations—addition, subtraction, multiplication, and division—that are useful for commercial transactions and in bookkeeping.

In modern terminology, the abacus is a digital device; that is, it represents values discretely. A bead is either in one predefined position or another, representing unambiguously, say, one or zero.

ANALOG CALCULATORS: FROM NAPIER'S LOGARITHMS TO THE SLIDE RULE

Calculating devices took a different turn when John Napier, a Scottish mathematician, published his discovery of logarithms in 1614. As any person can attest, adding two 10-digit numbers is much simpler than multiplying them together, and the transformation of a multiplication problem into an addition problem is exactly what logarithms enable. This simplification is possible because of the following logarithmic property: the logarithm of the product of two numbers is equal to the sum of the logarithms of the numbers. By 1624, tables with 14 significant digits were available for the logarithms of numbers from 1 to 20,000, and scientists quickly adopted the new labour-saving tool for tedious astronomical calculations.

Most significant for the development of computing, the transformation of multiplication into addition greatly simplified the possibility of mechanization. Analog calculating devices based on Napier's logarithms—representing digital values with analogous physical lengths—soon appeared. In 1620 Edmund Gunter, the English mathematician who coined the terms *cosine* and *cotangent*, built a device for performing navigational calculations: the Gunter scale, or, as navigators simply called it, the gunter. About 1632 an English clergyman and mathematician named William Oughtred built the first slide rule, drawing on Napier's ideas. That first slide rule was circular, but Oughtred also built the first rectangular one in 1633.

The analog devices of Gunter and Oughtred had various advantages and disadvantages compared with digital devices such as the abacus. What is important is that the consequences of these design decisions were being tested in the real world.

THE SLIDE RULE

During the 17th and 18th centuries, various mathematically and mechanically adroit men, mainly in Great Britain, contributed to the idea of taking two or more scales inscribed with numerical values and putting them in a device that allowed the scales to be moved relative to one another. By means of this movement, numbers on the scales might be matched up and calculations based on these numbers might be carried out mechanically.

John Napier is given credit for the invention (in 1614) of logarithms, which made it possible to simplify difficult mathematical problems and perform calculations on a printed table. A table is not a slide rule, but Napier's logarithms were a first step. Englishman Edmund Gunter devised the earliest known logarithmic rule (known as Gunter's scale, or the gunter), which aided seamen with nautical calculations. In 1632 another Englishman, William Oughtred, designed the first adjustable logarithmic rule. This one was circular, but Oughtred also designed the first linear slide rule. The familiar inner sliding rule was invented by an English instrument-maker, Robert Bissaker, in 1654.

The usefulness of the slide rule for rapid calculation was quickly recognized, and the instrument was made in considerable numbers, with slight modifications. Improvements in the direction of increased accuracy were initiated by Matthew Boulton and James Watt from about 1779 in connection with calculations in the design of steam engines at their works at Birmingham, Eng. In 1814, English physician Peter Roget (of *Roget's Thesaurus* fame) invented his "log-log" slide rule for calculating powers and roots of numbers. Amédée Mannheim, an officer of the French artillery, invented in 1859 what may be considered the first of the modern slide rules. This rule had scales on one face only. The Mannheim rule, which also brought into general use a cursor, or indicator, was much used in France, and after about 1880 it was imported in large numbers into other countries.

The most important of later improvements in the slide rule was the arrangement of the scales, trigonometric and log-log, so that they operated together while maintaining a consistent relationship to the basic scales. This arrangement gave added speed and flexibility to the solving of many problems—simple and complex alike—because it produced solutions by continuous operation instead of requiring the user to combine intermediate readings. The slide rule remained an essential tool in science and engineering until it was superseded by the portable electronic calculator late in the 20th century.

A member of Britain's WAAF (Women's Auxiliary Air Force) uses a slide rule for mathematical calculations during World War II. Keystone Features/Hulton Archive/Getty Images

Digital Calculators: From the Calculating Clock to the Arithmometer

In 1623 the German astronomer and mathematician Wilhelm Schickard built the first calculator. He described it in a letter to his friend the astronomer Johannes Kepler, and in 1624 he wrote again to explain that a machine he had commissioned to be built for Kepler was, apparently along with the prototype, destroyed in a fire. He called it a calculating clock, and modern engineers have been able to reproduce it from details in his letters. Even general knowledge of the clock had been temporarily lost when Schickard and his entire family perished during the Thirty Years' War.

But Schickard may not have been the true inventor of the calculator. A century earlier, Leonardo da Vinci sketched plans for a calculator that were sufficiently complete and correct for modern engineers to build a calculator on their basis.

The first calculator or adding machine to be produced in any quantity and actually used was the Pascaline, or arithmetic machine, designed and built by the French mathematician-philosopher Blaise Pascal between 1642 and 1644. It could only do addition and subtraction, with numbers being entered by manipulating its dials. Pascal invented the machine for his father, a tax collector, so it was the first business machine, too (if one does not count the abacus). He built 50 of them over the next 10 years.

In 1671 the German mathematician-philosopher Gottfried Wilhelm von Leibniz designed a calculating machine called the step reckoner. (It was first built in 1673.) The step reckoner expanded on Pascal's ideas and did multiplication by repeated addition and shifting.

Leibniz was a strong advocate of the binary number system. Binary numbers are ideal for machines because they require only two digits, which can easily be represented by the on and off states of a switch. When computers became electronic, the binary system was particularly appropriate because an electrical circuit is either on or off. This meant that on could represent true, off could represent false, and the flow of current would directly represent the flow of logic.

Leibniz was prescient in seeing the appropriateness of the binary system in calculating machines, but his machine did not use it. Instead, the step reckoner represented numbers in decimal form, as positions on 10-position dials. Even decimal representation was not a given: in 1668 Samuel Morland invented an adding machine specialized for British money—a decidedly nondecimal system.

Pascal's, Leibniz's, and Morland's devices were curiosities, but with the Industrial Revolution of the 18th century came a widespread need to perform repetitive operations efficiently. With other activities being mechanized, why not calculation? In 1820 Charles Xavier Thomas de Colmar of France effectively met this challenge when he built his arithmometer, the first commercial mass-produced calculating device. It could perform addition, subtraction, multiplication, and, with some more elaborate user involvement, division. Based on Leibniz's technology, it was extremely popular and sold for 90 years. In contrast to the modern calculator's credit-card size, the arithmometer was large enough to cover a desktop.

THE JACQUARD LOOM

Calculators such as the arithmometer remained a fascination after 1820, and their potential for commercial use was well understood. Many other mechanical devices built during the 19th century also performed repetitive functions more or less automatically, but few had any application to computing. There was one major exception: the Jacquard loom, invented in 1804–05 by a French weaver, Joseph-Marie Jacquard.

The Jacquard loom was a marvel of the Industrial Revolution. A textile-weaving loom, it could also be called the first practical information-processing device. The loom worked by tugging various-coloured threads into patterns by means of an array of rods. By inserting a card punched with holes, an operator could control the motion of the rods and thereby alter the pattern of the weave. But that was not all: the loom was also equipped with a card-reading

Jacquard loom, engraving, 1874. At the top of the machine is a stack of punched cards that would be fed into the loom to control the weaving pattern. This method of automatically issuing machine instructions was employed by computers well into the 20th century. The Bettmann Archive

device that slipped a new card from a prepunched deck into place every time the shuttle was thrown so that complex weaving patterns could be automated.

What was extraordinary about the device was that it transferred the design process from a labour-intensive weaving stage to a card-punching stage. Once the cards had been punched and assembled, the design was complete, and the loom implemented the design automatically. The Jacquard loom, therefore, could be said to be programmed for different patterns by these decks of punched cards.

For those intent on mechanizing calculations, the Jacquard loom provided important lessons: the sequence of operations that a machine performs could be controlled to make the machine do something quite different; a punched card could be used as a medium for directing the machine; and, most important, a device could be directed to perform different tasks by feeding it instructions in a sort of language—i.e., making the machine programmable.

It is not too great a stretch to say that, in the Jacquard loom, programming was invented before the computer. The close relationship between the device and the program became apparent some 20 years later, with Charles Babbage's invention of the first computer.

THE FIRST COMPUTER

By the second decade of the 19th century, a number of ideas necessary for the invention of the computer were in the air. First, the potential benefits to science and industry of being able to automate routine calculations were appreciated, as they had not been a century earlier. Specific methods to make automated calculation more practical, such as doing multiplication by adding logarithms or by repeating addition, had been invented, and experience with both analog and digital devices had shown some of the benefits of each approach. The Jacquard loom had shown the benefits of directing a multipurpose device through coded instructions, and it had demonstrated how punched cards could be used to modify those instructions quickly and flexibly. It was a mathematical genius in England who began to put all these pieces together.

THE DIFFERENCE ENGINE

Charles Babbage was an English mathematician and inventor: he invented the cowcatcher, reformed the British postal system, and was a pioneer in the fields of operations research and actuarial science. It was Babbage who first suggested that the weather of years past could be read from tree rings. He also had a lifelong fascination with keys, ciphers, and mechanical dolls.

As a founding member of the Royal Astronomical Society, Babbage had seen a clear need to design and build a mechanical device that could automate long, tedious astronomical calculations. He began by writing a letter in 1822 to Sir Humphry Davy, president of the Royal Society, about the possibility of automating the construction of mathematical tables—specifically, logarithm tables for use in navigation. He then wrote a paper, "On the Theoretical Principles of the Machinery for Calculating Tables," which he read to the society later that year. (It won the Royal Society's first Gold Medal in 1823.) Tables then in use often contained errors, which could be a life-and-death matter for sailors at sea, and Babbage argued that, by automating the production of the tables, he could assure their accuracy. Having gained support in the society for his difference engine, as he called it, Babbage next turned to the British government to fund development, obtaining one of the world's first government grants for research and technological development.

Babbage approached the project very seriously: he hired a master machinist, set up a fireproof workshop, and built a dustproof environment for testing the device. Up until then calculations were rarely carried out to more than 6 digits; Babbage planned to produce 20- or 30-digit results routinely. The difference engine was a digital device: it operated on discrete digits rather than smooth quantities, and the digits were decimal (0–9), represented by positions on toothed wheels, rather than the binary digits that Leibniz favoured (but did not use). When one of the toothed wheels turned from 9 to 0, it caused the next wheel to advance one position, carrying the digit just as Leibniz's step reckoner calculator had operated.

The difference engine was more than a simple calculator, however. It mechanized not just a single calculation but a whole series of calculations on a number of variables to solve a complex problem. It went far beyond calculators in other ways as well. Like modern computers, the difference engine had storage—that is, a place where data could be held temporarily for later processing—and it was designed to stamp its output into soft metal, which could later be used to produce a printing plate.

Nevertheless, the difference engine performed only one operation. The operator would set up all of its data registers with the original data, and then the single operation would be repeatedly applied to all of the registers, ultimately producing a solution. Still, in complexity and audacity of design, it dwarfed any calculating device then in existence.

The full engine, designed to be room-size, was never built, at least not by Babbage. Although he sporadically received several government grants—governments changed, funding often ran out, and he had to personally bear some of the financial costs—he was working at or near the tolerances of the construction methods of the day, and he ran into numerous construction difficulties. All design and construction ceased in 1833, when Joseph Clement, the machinist responsible for actually building the machine, refused to continue unless he was prepaid. (The completed portion of the difference engine is on permanent exhibition today at the Science Museum in London.)

THE ANALYTICAL ENGINE

While working on the difference engine, Babbage began to imagine ways to improve it. Chiefly he thought about generalizing its operation so that it could perform other kinds of calculations. By the time the funding had run out in 1833, he had conceived of something far more

This trial portion of Difference Engine No. 1 was assembled in 1832 by Charles Babbage's engineer, Joseph Clement. It consists of about 2,000 parts and represents one-seventh of the complete engine. SSPL via Getty Images

revolutionary: a general-purpose computing machine called the analytical engine.

The analytical engine was to be a general-purpose, fully program-controlled, automatic mechanical digital computer. It would be able to perform any calculation set before it. Before Babbage there is no evidence that anyone had ever conceived of such a device, let alone attempted to build one. The machine was designed to consist of four components: the mill, the store, the reader, and the printer. These components are the essential components of every computer today. The mill was the calculating unit, analogous to the central processing unit (CPU) in a modern computer; the store was where data were held prior to processing, exactly analogous to memory and storage in today's computers; and the reader and printer were the input and output devices.

As with the difference engine, the project was far more complex than anything built before. The store was to be large enough to hold 1,000 50-digit numbers; this was larger than the storage capacity of any computer built before 1960. The machine was to be steam-driven and run by one attendant. The printing capability was also ambitious, as it had been for the difference engine: Babbage wanted to automate the process as much as possible, right up to producing printed tables of numbers.

The reader was another new feature of the analytical engine. Data (numbers) were to be entered on punched cards, using the card-reading technology of the Jacquard loom. Instructions were also to be entered on cards, another idea taken directly from Jacquard. The use of instruction cards would make it a programmable device and far more flexible than any machine then in existence. Another element of programmability was to be its ability to execute instructions in other than sequential order. It was to have a kind of decision-making ability in its conditional control transfer, also known as conditional branching, whereby it would be able to jump to a different instruction depending on the value of some data. This extremely powerful feature was missing in many of the early computers of the 20th century.

By most definitions, the wngine was a real computer as understood today—or would have been, had not Babbage run into implementation problems again. Actually building his ambitious design was judged infeasible given the current technology, and Babbage's failure to generate the promised mathematical tables with his difference engine had dampened enthusiasm for further government funding. Indeed, it was apparent to the British government that Babbage was more interested in innovation than in constructing tables.

All the same, Babbage's Analytical Engine was something new under the sun. Its most revolutionary feature was the ability to change its operation by changing the instructions on punched cards. Until this breakthrough, all the mechanical aids to calculation were merely calculators or, like the difference engine, glorified calculators. The analytical engine, although not actually completed, was the first machine that deserved to be called a computer.

One feature of the analytical engine was its ability to place numbers and instructions temporarily in its store and return them to its mill for processing at an appropriate time. This was accomplished by the proper sequencing of instructions and data in its reader, and the ability to reorder instructions and data gave the machine a flexibility and power that was hard to grasp. The first electronic digital computers of a century later lacked this ability. It would be 100 years before anyone would understand it so well again. In the intervening century, attention would be diverted to the calculator and other business machines.

LADY LOVELACE: THE FIRST PROGRAMMER

The distinction between calculator and computer, although clear to Babbage, was not apparent to most people in the early 19th century, even to the intellectually adventuresome visitors at Babbage's soirees—with the exception of a young girl of unusual parentage and education.

Augusta Ada King, the Countess of Lovelace, was the daughter of the poet Lord Byron and the mathematically inclined Anne

Augusta Ada King,, Countess of Lovelace. Hulton Archive/Getty Images

Millbanke. One of her tutors was Augustus De Morgan, a famous mathematician and logician. Because Byron was involved in a notorious scandal at the time of her birth, Ada's mother encouraged her mathematical and scientific interests, hoping to suppress any inclination to wildness she may have inherited from her father.

Toward that end, Lady Lovelace attended Babbage's soirees and became fascinated with his difference engine. She also corresponded with him, asking pointed questions. It was his plan for the Analytical Engine that truly fired her imagination, however. In 1843, at age 27, she had come to understand it well enough to publish the definitive paper explaining the device and drawing the crucial distinction between this new thing and existing calculators. The analytical engine, she argued, went beyond the bounds of arithmetic. Because it operated on general symbols rather than on numbers, it established "a link...between the operations of matter and the abstract mental processes of the most abstract branch of mathematical science." It was a physical device that was capable of operating in the realm of abstract thought.

Lady Lovelace rightly reported that this was not only something no one had built, it was something that no one before had even conceived. She went on to become the world's only expert on the process of sequencing instructions on the punched cards that the analytical engine used; that is, she became the world's first computer programmer.

EARLY BUSINESS MACHINES

Throughout the 19th century, business machines were coming into common use. Calculators became available as a tool of commerce with the appearance of Colmar's arithmometer (described previously) in 1820, and in 1874 the Remington Arms Company, Inc., sold the first commercially viable typewriter. Other machines were invented for other specific business tasks. None of these machines was a computer, but they did advance the state of practical mechanical knowledge—knowledge that would be used in computers later.

HERMAN HOLLERITH'S CENSUS TABULATOR

One of these machines was invented in response to a sort of constitutional crisis in the United States: the census tabulator. The U.S. Constitution mandates that a census of the population be performed every 10 years. The first attempt at any mechanization of the census was in 1870, when statistical data were transcribed onto a rolling paper tape displayed through a small slotted window. As the size of America's population exploded in the 19th century and the number of census questions expanded, the urgency of further mechanization became increasingly clear.

After graduating from the Columbia University School of Mines, New York City, in 1879, Herman Hollerith obtained his first job with one of his former professors, William P. Trowbridge, who had received a commission as a special agent for the 1880 census. It was while employed at the Census Office that Hollerith first saw the pressing need for automating the tabulation of statistical data.

Over the next 10 years Hollerith refined his ideas, obtaining his first patent in 1884 for a machine to punch and count cards. He then organized the health records for Baltimore, Md., for New York City, and for the state of New Jersey—all in preparation for winning the contract to tabulate the 1890 U.S. Census. The success of the U.S. Census opened European governments to Hollerith's machines. Most notably, a contract with the Russian government, signed on Dec. 15, 1896, may have induced him to incorporate as the Tabulating Machine Company on Dec. 5, 1896.

OTHER EARLY BUSINESS MACHINE COMPANIES

Improvements in calculators continued: by the 1880s they could add in the accumulation of partial results, store

The Hollerith tabulator and sorter box, invented by Herman Hollerith and used in the 1890 U.S. Census. It "read" cards by passing them through electrical contacts. Hulton Archive/Getty Images

past results, and print. Then, in 1892, William Seward Burroughs, who along with two other St. Louis, Mo., businessmen had started the American Arithmometer Company in 1886 in order to build adding machines, obtained a patent for one of the first truly practical and commercially successful calculators. Burroughs died in 1898, and his company was reorganized as the Burroughs Adding Machine Company in Detroit, Mich., in 1905.

All the calculators—and virtually all the information-processing devices—sold at this time were designed for commercial purposes, not scientific research. By the turn of the century, commercial calculating devices were in common use, as were other special-purpose machines such as one that generated serial numbers for banknotes. As a result, many of the business machine companies in the United States were doing well, including Hollerith's Tabulating Machine Company.

In 1911 several of these companies combined to form the Computing-Tabulating-Recording Company, or CTR. In 1914 Thomas J. Watson, Sr., left his sales manager position at the National Cash Register Company to become president of CTR, and 10 years later CTR changed its name to International Business Machines Corporation, or IBM. In the second half of the century, IBM would become the giant of the world computer industry, but such commercial gains did not take place until enormous progress had been made in the theoretical understanding of the modern computer during the remarkable decades of the 1930s and '40s.

CHAPTER 2

INVENTION OF THE MODERN COMPUTER

The true power of computing came to be realized in the 20th century, but in order to realize that great dream, inventors had to learn that the thing they were trying to invent was not just a number cruncher, not merely a calculator like Herman Hollerith's and William Seward Burroughs's adding machines. They had to learn, for example, that it was not necessary to invent a new computer for every new calculation: a computer could be designed to solve numerous problems, even problems not yet imagined when the computer was built. Inventors also had to learn how to tell such a general problem-solving computer which problem to solve. In other words, they had to invent programming. Then they had to solve all the heady problems of developing such a device, of implementing the design, and of actually building the thing.

EARLY EXPERIMENTS

As the technology for realizing a computer was being honed by the business machine companies in the early 20th century, the theoretical foundations were being laid in academia. During the 1930s two important strains of computer-related research were being pursued in the United States at two universities in Cambridge, Mass. One strain produced the differential analyzer, the other a series of devices ending with the Harvard Mark IV. Meanwhile, across the Atlantic at the University of Cambridge, a young mathematician articulated the concept of a universal computing device, now known as the Turing machine.

VANNEVAR BUSH'S DIFFERENTIAL ANALYZER

In 1930 an engineer named Vannevar Bush at the Massachusetts Institute of Technology (MIT) developed the first modern analog computer. The differential analyzer, as he called it, was an analog calculator that could be used to solve certain classes of differential equations, a type of problem common in physics and engineering applications that is often very tedious to solve. Variables were represented by shaft motion, and addition and multiplication were accomplished by feeding the values into a set of gears. Integration was carried out by means of a knife-edged wheel rotating at a variable radius on a circular

The machine s... ...ere is half of the original Differential Analyzer. It was based on the Differential Analyzer built in 1930 by Vannevar Bush at the Massachusetts Institute of Technology (MIT). SSPL via Getty Images

table. The individual mechanical integrators were then interconnected to solve a set of differential equations.

The differential analyzer proved highly useful, and a number of them were built and used at various universities. Still the device was limited to solving this one class of problem, and, as is the case for all analog devices, it produced approximate, albeit practical, solutions. Nevertheless, important applications for analog computers and analog-digital hybrid computers still exist, particularly for simulating complicated dynamical systems such as aircraft flight, nuclear power plant operations, and chemical reactions.

Howard Aiken's Digital Calculators

While Bush was working on analog computing at MIT, across town Harvard professor Howard Aiken was working with digital devices for calculation. He had begun to realize in hardware something like Babbage's analytical engine, which he had read about. Starting in 1937, he laid out detailed plans for a series of four calculating machines of increasing sophistication, based on different technologies.

Aiken was methodically exploring the technological advances made since the mechanical assembly and steam power available to Babbage. Electromagnetic relay circuits were already being used in business machines, and the vacuum tube—a switch with no moving parts, very high speed action, and greater reliability than electro-mechanical relays—was quickly put to use in the early experimental machines.

The business machines of the time used plugboards (something like telephone switchboards) to route data manually, and Aiken chose not to use them for the specification of instructions. This turned out to make his machine much easier to program than the more famous ENIAC, designed somewhat later, which had to be manually rewired for each program.

From 1939 to 1944 Aiken, in collaboration with IBM, developed his first fully functional computer, known as the Harvard Mark I. The machine, like Babbage's, was huge: more than 50 feet (15 metres) long, weighing 5 tons, and consisting of about 750,000 separate parts, it was mostly mechanical. For input and output it used three paper-tape readers, two card readers, a card punch, and two typewriters. It took between three and six seconds to add two

View of IBM's Harvard Mark I, also called the Automatic Sequence Controlled Calculator, on the campus of Harvard University, Cambridge, Mass., 1944. PhotoQuest/Archive Photos/Getty Images

numbers. Aiken developed three more such machines (Mark II–IV) over the next few years and is credited with developing the first fully automatic large-scale calculator.

The Turing Machine

Alan Turing, a mathematics student at the University of Cambridge, was inspired by German mathematician David Hilbert's formalist program, which sought to demonstrate that any mathematical problem can potentially be solved by an algorithm—that is, by a purely mechanical process. Turing interpreted this to mean a computing machine and set out to design one capable of resolving all mathematical problems, but in the process he proved in his seminal paper "On Computable Numbers, with an Application to the *Entscheidungsproblem* ['Halting Problem']" (1936) that no such universal mathematical solver could ever exist.

In order to design his machine (known to posterity as the "Turing machine"), he needed to find an unambiguous definition of the essence of a computer. In doing so, Turing worked out in great detail the basic concepts of a universal computing machine—that is, a computing machine that could, at least in theory, do anything that a special-purpose computing device could do. In particular, it would not be limited to doing arithmetic. The internal states of the machine could represent numbers, but they could equally well represent logic values or letters. In fact, Turing believed that everything could be represented symbolically, even abstract mental states, and he was one of the first advocates of the artificial-intelligence position that computers can potentially "think."

Turing's work up to this point was entirely abstract, entirely a theoretical demonstration. Nevertheless, he made it clear from the start that his results implied the

THE TURING TEST

In 1950 Alan Turing made a major contribution to the emerging field of artificial intelligence by proposing a simple method for determining whether a computer could actually "think." Sidestepping the debate about exactly how to define "thinking," he suggested a very practical, albeit subjective, standard: if a computer acts, reacts, and interacts like a sentient being, then call it sentient. In what Turing called the "imitation game" (now known as the Turing test), a remote human interrogator, within a fixed time frame, would have to distinguish between a computer and a human subject based on their replies to various questions posed by the interrogator. If the computer was misidentified as the human subject in a certain percentage of such questions in a series of such tests, it could be said to be "thinking." Turing predicted that by the year 2000 a computer "would be able to play the imitation game so well that an average interrogator will not have more than a 70-percent chance of making the right identification (machine or human) after five minutes of questioning."

In 1991 the American philanthropist Hugh Loebner started the annual Loebner Prize competition, promising a $100,000 payout to the first computer to pass the Turing test and awarding $2,000 each year to the best effort. With the year 2000 more than a full decade past, no program has come close to passing an undiluted Turing test.

possibility of building a machine of the sort he described. His work characterized the abstract essence of any computing device so well that it was in effect a challenge to actually build one.

Turing's work had an immediate effect on only a small number of academics at a few universities who were interested in the concept of computing machinery. It had no immediate effect on the growing industry of business machines, all of which were special-purpose devices. But to the few who were interested, Turing's work was an inspiration to pursue something of which most of the world had not even conceived: a universal computing machine.

PIONEERING WORK

Aside from the theoretical work being done at the two Cambridges, the hard practical work of translating designs into actual built machines was attempted in the 1930s and early 1940s, before World War II put a stop to some work (though giving a boost to other work).

The Atanasoff-Berry Computer

It is generally believed that the first electronic digital computers were the wartime Colossus, built in England in 1943, and the ENIAC, built in the United States in 1945 (see below). However, the first special-purpose electronic computer may actually have been invented by John Vincent Atanasoff, a physicist and mathematician at Iowa State College (now Iowa State University), during 1937–42. Together with his graduate assistant Clifford E. Berry, Atanasoff built a successful small prototype in 1939 for the purpose of testing two ideas central to his design: capacitors to store data in binary form and electronic logic circuits to perform addition and subtraction. They then began the design and construction of a larger, more general-purpose computer, now known as the Atanasoff-Berry Computer, or ABC.

Various components of the ABC were designed and built from 1939 to 1942, but development was discontinued with the entry of the United States into World War II. The ABC featured about 300 vacuum tubes for control and arithmetic calculations, use of binary numbers, logic operations (instead of direct counting), memory capacitors, and punched cards as input/output units. At Atanasoff's invitation, another early computer pioneer, John Mauchly, stayed at his home and was freely shown

Clifford Berry and the Atanasoff-Berry Computer. The ABC, c. 1942, was possibly the first electronic digital computer. Iowa State University Photo Service

his work for several days in June 1941. This visit may have been important in the development of ENIAC.

The First Computer Network

Between 1940 and 1946 George Stibitz and his team at Bell Laboratories built a series of machines with telephone technologies—i.e., employing electromechanical relays. These were the first machines to serve more than one user and the first to work remotely over telephone lines. However, because they were based on slow mechanical relays rather than electronic switches, they became obsolete almost as soon as they were constructed.

Konrad Zuse

Meanwhile, in Germany, engineer Konrad Zuse had been thinking about calculating machines. He was advised by a calculator manufacturer in 1937 that the field was a dead end and that every computing problem had already been solved. Zuse had something else in mind, though.

For one thing, Zuse worked in binary from the beginning. All of his prototype machines, built in 1936, used binary representation in order to simplify construction. This had the added advantage of making the connection with logic clearer, and Zuse worked out the details of how the operations of logic (e.g., AND, OR, and NOT) could be mapped onto the design of the computer's circuits. (English mathematician George Boole had shown the connection between logic and mathematics in the mid-19th century, developing an algebra of logic now known as Boolean algebra.) Zuse also spent more time than his predecessors and contemporaries developing software for his computer, the language in which it was to be programmed. Although all his early prewar machines were really calculators—not computers—his Z3, completed in December 1941 (and destroyed on April 6, 1945, during an Allied air raid on Berlin), was the first program-controlled processor.

Because all Zuse's work was done in relative isolation, he knew little about work on computers in the United States and England, and, when the war began, the isolation became complete.

DEVELOPMENTS DURING WORLD WAR II

The exigencies of war gave impetus and funding to computer research. In Britain the impetus was code breaking. In Germany, Konrad Zuse received funding from the Air Ministry. In the United States, government funding supported the use of computers for the development of a range of weaponry, from artillery to nuclear bombs. Some of these efforts resulted in the development of the first fully functional digital computers.

COLOSSUS

In wartime Britain the Ultra project was funded with much secrecy to develop the technology necessary to crack ciphers and codes produced by the German electromechanical devices known as the Enigma and the Geheimschreiber ("Secret Writer"). The first in a series of important code-breaking machines, Colossus, also known as the Mark I, was built under the direction of Sir Thomas Flowers and delivered in December 1943 to the code-breaking operation at Bletchley Park, a government research centre north of London. It employed approximately 1,800 vacuum tubes for computations. Successively larger and more elaborate versions were built over the next two years.

Although it lacked some characteristics now associated with computers, Colossus can plausibly be described as the first electronic digital computer, and it was certainly a key stepping-stone to the development of the modern computer. Although Colossus was designed to perform specific cryptographic-related calculations, it could be used for more-generalized purposes. Its design pioneered the massive use of electronics in computation, and it

Members of Britain's Women's Royal Naval Service working on Colossus, the world's first electronic programmable computer, at Britain's Bletchley Park in 1943. Bletchley Park Trust/SSPL/Getty Images

embodied an insight from Flowers of the importance of storing data electronically within the machine. The operation at Bletchley foreshadowed the modern data centre.

Colossus was successful in its intended purpose: the German messages it helped to decode provided information about German battle orders, supplies, and personnel; it also confirmed that an Allied deception campaign, Operation Fortitude, was working. The series of Colossus computers were disassembled after the war, and most information about them remained classified until the 1990s. In 1996 the basic Colossus machine was rebuilt and switched on at Bletchley Park, which is now a museum open to the public.

The Ultra project had a gifted mathematician associated with the Bletchley Park effort, and one familiar with codes. Alan Turing may have pushed the project further in the direction of a general-purpose device than his government originally had in mind. Turing's advocacy helped keep up government support for the project.

THE Z4

In Germany, Konrad Zuse began construction of the Z4 in 1943. Like Zuse's Z3, the Z4 used electromechanical relays, in part because of the difficulty in acquiring the roughly 2,000 necessary vacuum tubes in wartime Germany. The Z4 was evacuated from Berlin in early 1945, and it eventually wound up in Hinterstein, a small village in the Bavarian Alps, where it remained until Zuse brought it to the Federal Technical Institute in Zürich, Switz., for refurbishing in 1950. Although unable to continue with hardware development, Zuse made a number of advances in software design.

Zuse's use of floating-point representation for numbers—the significant digits, known as the mantissa, are stored separately from a pointer to the decimal point, known as the exponent, allowing a very large range of numbers to be handled—was far ahead of its time. In addition, Zuse developed a rich set of instructions, handled infinite values correctly, and included a "no-op"—that is, an instruction that did nothing. Only significant experience in programming would show the need for something so apparently useless.

The Z4's program was punched on used movie film and was separate from the mechanical memory for data (in other words, there was no stored program). The machine was relatively reliable (it normally ran all night unattended), but it had no decision-making ability. Addition took 0.5 to 1.25 seconds, multiplication 3.5 seconds.

ENIAC

In the United States, government funding went to a project led by John Mauchly, J. Presper Eckert, Jr., and their colleagues at the Moore School of Electrical Engineering at the University of Pennsylvania; their objective was an all-electronic computer. Under contract to the army and under the direction of Herman Goldstine, work began in early 1943 on the Electronic Numerical Integrator and Computer (ENIAC). The next year, mathematician John von Neumann, already on full-time leave from the Institute for Advanced Studies (IAS), Princeton, N.J., for various government research projects (including the Manhattan Project), began frequent consultations with the group.

ENIAC was something less than the dream of a universal computer. Designed for the specific purpose of computing values for artillery range tables, it lacked some features that would have made it a more generally useful machine. Like Colossus but unlike Howard Aiken's Harvard Mark I, it used plugboards for communicating instructions to the machine; this had the advantage that, once the instructions were thus "programmed," the machine ran at electronic speed. Instructions read from a card reader or other slow mechanical device would not have been able to keep up with the all-electronic ENIAC. The disadvantage was that it took days to rewire the machine for each new problem. This was such a liability that only with some generosity could it be called programmable.

Nevertheless, ENIAC was the most powerful calculating device built to date. Like Charles Babbage's analytical engine and the Colossus, but unlike Aiken's Mark I, Konrad Zuse's Z4, and George Stibitz's telephone-savvy machine, it did have conditional branching—that is, it had the ability to execute different instructions or to alter the order of execution of instructions based on the value of some data. (For instance, IF X > 5 THEN GO TO LINE 23.) This gave ENIAC a lot of flexibility and meant that, while it was built for a specific purpose, it could be used for a wider range of problems.

ENIAC was enormous. It occupied the 50-by-30-foot (15-by-9-metre) basement of the Moore School, where its 40 panels were arranged, U-shaped, along three walls. Each of the units was about 2 feet wide by 2 feet deep by 8 feet high (0.6 by 0.6 by 2.4 metres). With approximately

American engineers John Mauchly and J. Presper Eckert, Jr., as seen here in the 1960s looking at a portion of ENIAC (Electronic Numerical Integrator and Computer), which they codesigned in 1946. Hulton Archive/Getty Images

18,000 vacuum tubes, 70,000 resistors, 10,000 capacitors, 6,000 switches, and 1,500 relays, it was easily the most complex electronic system ever built to that time. ENIAC ran continuously (in part to extend tube life), generating 150 kilowatts of heat, and could execute up to 5,000 additions per second, several orders of magnitude faster than its electromechanical predecessors.

Completed by February 1946, ENIAC had cost the government $400,000, and the war it was designed to help win was over. Its first task was doing calculations for the construction of a hydrogen bomb. A portion of the machine is on exhibit today at the Smithsonian Institution in Washington, D.C.

TOWARD THE CLASSICAL COMPUTER

The computers built during the war were built under unusual constraints. The British work was largely focused on code breaking, the American work on computing projectile trajectories and calculations for the atomic bomb. The computers were built as special-purpose devices, although they often embodied more general-purpose computing capabilities than their specifications called for. The vacuum tubes in these machines were not entirely reliable, but with no moving parts they were more reliable than the electromechanical switches they replaced, and they were much faster. Reliability was an issue, since Colossus used some 1,500 tubes and ENIAC on the order of 18,000. But ENIAC was, by virtue of its electronic realization, 1,000 times faster than the Harvard Mark I. Such speed meant that the machine could perform calculations that were theretofore beyond human ability.

Colossus, ENIAC, and subsequent computers employing vacuum tubes are known as first-generation computers. (With 1,500 mechanical relays, ENIAC was still transitional to later, fully electronic computers.) Although tubes were a great advance over the electromechanical realization of Aiken or the steam-and-mechanical model of Babbage, the basic architecture of the machines (that is, the functions they were able to perform) was not much advanced beyond Babbage's difference engine and analytical engine. In fact, the original name for ENIAC was Electronic Difference Analyzer, and it was built to perform much like Babbage's difference engine. After the war, efforts focused on fulfilling the grander idea of a general-purpose computing device.

EDVAC's Bigger Brains

In 1945, before ENIAC was even finished, planning began at the Moore School for ENIAC's successor, the Electronic Discrete Variable Automatic Computer, or EDVAC. ENIAC was hampered, as all previous electronic computers had been, by the need to use one vacuum tube to store each bit, or binary digit. The feasible number of vacuum tubes in a computer also posed a practical limit on storage capacity—beyond a certain point, vacuum tubes are bound to burn out as fast as they can be changed. For EDVAC, Eckert had a new idea for storage.

In 1880 French physicists Pierre and Jacques Curie had discovered that applying an electric current to a quartz crystal would produce a characteristic vibration and vice versa. During the 1930s at Bell Laboratories, William Shockley, later coinventor of the transistor, had demonstrated a device—a tube, called a delay line, containing water and ethylene glycol—for effecting a predictable delay in information transmission. Eckert had already built and experimented in 1943 with such a delay line (using mercury) in conjunction with radar research, and sometime in 1944 he hit upon the new idea of placing a quartz crystal at each end of the mercury delay line in order to sustain and modify the resulting pattern. In effect, he invented a new storage device. Whereas ENIAC required one tube per bit, EDVAC could use a delay line and 10 vacuum tubes to store 1,000 bits. Before the invention of the magnetic core memory and the transistor, which would eliminate the need for vacuum tubes altogether, the mercury delay line was instrumental in increasing computer storage and reliability.

Von Neumann's "Preliminary Discussion"

But the design of the modern, or classical, computer did not fully crystallize until the publication of a 1946 paper by Arthur Burks, Herman Goldstine, and John von Neumann titled "Preliminary Discussion of the Logical Design of an Electronic Computing Instrument." Although the paper was essentially a synthesis of ideas currently in the air, it is frequently cited as the birth certificate of computer science.

Among the principles enunciated in the paper were that data and instructions should be kept in a single store and that instructions should be encoded so as to be modifiable by other instructions. This was an extremely critical decision because it meant that one program could be treated as data by another program. Zuse had considered and rejected this possibility as too dangerous. But its inclusion by von Neumann's group made possible high-level programming languages and most of the advances in software of the following 50 years. Subsequently, computers with stored programs would be known as von Neumann machines.

One problem that the stored-program idea solved was the need for rapid access to instructions. Colossus and

ENIAC had used plugboards, which had the advantage of enabling the instructions to be read in electronically, rather than by much slower mechanical card readers, but it also had the disadvantage of making these first-generation machines very hard to program. But if the instructions could be stored in the same electronic memory that held the data, they could be accessed as quickly as needed. One immediately obvious consequence was that EDVAC would need a lot more memory than ENIAC.

THE FIRST STORED-PROGRAM MACHINES

Government secrecy hampered British efforts to build on wartime computer advances, but engineers in Britain still beat the Americans to the goal of building the first stored-program digital computer. At the University of Manchester, Frederic C. Williams and Tom Kilburn built a simple stored-program computer, known as the Baby, in 1948. This was built to test their invention of a way to store information on a cathode-ray tube that enabled direct access (in contrast to the mercury delay line's sequential access) to stored information. Although faster than Eckert's storage method, it proved somewhat unreliable. Nevertheless, it became the preferred storage method for most of the early computers worldwide that were not already committed to mercury delay lines.

By 1949 Williams and Kilburn had extended the Baby to a full-size computer, the Manchester Mark I. This had two major new features that were to become computer standards: a two-level store and instruction modification registers (which soon evolved into index registers). A magnetic drum was added to provide a random-access secondary storage device. Until machines were fitted with index registers, every instruction that referred to an address that varied as the program ran—e.g., an array element—had to be preceded by instructions to alter its address to the current required value. Four months after the Baby first worked, the British government contracted the electronics firm of Ferranti to build a production computer based on the prospective Mark I. This became the Ferranti Mark I—the first commercial computer—of which nine were sold.

Kilburn, Williams, and colleagues at Manchester also came up with a breakthrough that would revolutionize how a computer executed instructions: they made it possible for the address portion of an instruction to be modified while the program was running. Before this, an instruction specified that a particular action—say, addition—was to be performed on data in one or more particular locations. Their innovation allowed the location to be modified as part of the operation of executing the instruction. This made it very easy to address elements within an array sequentially.

At the University of Cambridge, meanwhile, Maurice Wilkes and others built what is recognized as the first full-size, fully electronic, stored-program computer to provide a formal computing service for users. The Electronic Delay Storage Automatic Calculator (EDSAC) was built on the set of principles synthesized by von Neumann and, like the Manchester Mark I, became operational in 1949. Wilkes built the machine chiefly to study programming issues, which he realized would become as important as the hardware details.

WHIRLWIND

New hardware continued to be invented, though. In the United States, Jay Forrester of the Massachusetts Institute of Technology (MIT) and Jan Aleksander Rajchman of the Radio Corporation of America (RCA) came up with a new kind of memory based on magnetic cores that was fast enough to enable MIT to build the first real-time computer, Whirlwind. A real-time computer is one that can respond seemingly instantly to basic instructions, thus allowing an operator to interact with a "running" computer.

UNIVAC

After leaving the Moore School, Eckert and Mauchly struggled to obtain capital to build their latest design, a computer they called the Universal Automatic Computer,

U.S. Air Force technicians in 1951 evaluate the UNIVAC computer system, which took up 352 square feet of floor space. Getty Images

or UNIVAC. (In the meantime, they contracted with the Northrop Corporation to build the Binary Automatic Computer, or BINAC, which, when completed in 1949, became the first American stored-program computer.) The partners delivered the first UNIVAC to the U.S. Bureau of the Census in March 1951, although their company, their patents, and their talents had been acquired by Remington Rand, Inc., in 1950. Although it owed something to experience with ENIAC, UNIVAC was built from the start as a stored-program computer, so it was really different architecturally. It used an operator keyboard and console typewriter for input and magnetic tape for all other input and output. Printed output was recorded on tape and then printed by a separate tape printer.

The UNIVAC I was designed as a commercial data-processing computer, intended to replace the punched-card accounting machines of the day. It could read 7,200 decimal digits per second (it did not use binary numbers), making it by far the fastest business machine yet built. Its use of Eckert's mercury delay lines greatly reduced the number of vacuum tubes needed (to 5,000), thus enabling the main processor to occupy a "mere" 14.5 by 7.5 by 9 feet (approximately 4.4 by 2.3 by 2.7 metres) of space. It was a true business machine, signaling the convergence of academic computational research with the office automation trend of the late 19th and early 20th centuries. As such, it ushered in the era of "Big Iron"—or large, mass-produced computing equipment.

CHAPTER 3

THE AGE OF BIG IRON

A snapshot of computer development in the early 1950s would have to show a number of companies and laboratories in competition—technological competition and increasingly earnest business competition—to produce the few computers then demanded for scientific research. Several computer-building projects had been launched immediately after the end of World War II in 1945, primarily in the United States and Britain. These projects were inspired chiefly by a 1946 document, "Preliminary Discussion of the Logical Design of an Electronic Digital Computing Instrument," produced by a group working under the direction of mathematician John von Neumann of the Institute for Advanced Study at Princeton University. The IAS paper, as von Neumann's document became known, articulated the concept of the stored program—a concept that has been called the single largest innovation in the history of the computer. Most computers built in the years following the paper's distribution were designed according to its plan, yet by 1950 there were still only a handful of working stored-program computers.

Business use at this time was marginal because the machines were so hard to use. Although computer makers such as Remington Rand, the Burroughs Adding Machine Company, and IBM had begun building machines to the IAS specifications, it was not until 1954 that a real market for business computers began to emerge. The IBM 650, delivered at the end of 1954 for colleges and businesses, was a decimal implementation of the IAS design. With this low-cost magnetic drum computer, which sold for about

Close-up of magnetic drum of IBM computer translator. Magnetic drums are precursors of hard disks, invented in 1956. Al Fenn/Time & Life Pictures/ Getty Images

$200,000 apiece (compared with about $1,000,000 for the scientific model, the IBM 701), IBM had a hit, eventually selling about 1,800 of them.

In addition, by offering universities that taught computer science courses around the IBM 650 an academic discount program (with price reductions of up to 60 percent), IBM established a cadre of engineers and programmers for their machines. (Apple later used a similar discount strategy in American grade schools to capture a large proportion of the early microcomputer market.)

A snapshot of the era would also have to show what could be called the sociology of computing. The actual use of computers was restricted to a small group of trained experts, and there was resistance to the idea that this group should be expanded by making the machines easier to use. Machine time was expensive, more expensive than the time of the mathematicians and scientists who needed to use the machines, and computers could process only one problem at a time. As a result, the machines were in a sense held in higher regard than the scientists. If a task could be done by a person, it was thought that the machine's time should not be wasted with it. The public's perception of computers was not positive either. If motion pictures of the time can be used as a guide, the popular image was of a room-filling brain attended by white-coated technicians, mysterious and somewhat frightening—about to eliminate jobs through automation.

THE NEED FOR PROGRAMMING LANGUAGES

Yet the machines of the early 1950s were not much more capable than Charles Babbage's analytical engine of the 1830s (although they were much faster). Although in principle these were general-purpose computers, they were still largely restricted to doing tough math problems. They often lacked the means to perform logical operations, and they had little text-handling capability—for example, lowercase letters were not even representable in the machines, even if there were devices capable of printing them. Also, the machines could be operated only by experts, and preparing a problem for computation (what would be called programming today) took a long time. With only one person at a time able to use a machine, major bottlenecks were created. Problems lined up like experiments waiting for a cyclotron or the space shuttle. Much of the machine's precious time was wasted because of this one-at-a-time protocol.

In sum, the machines were expensive and the market was still small. To be useful in a broader business market or even in a broader scientific market, computers would need application programs: word processors, database programs, and so on. These applications in turn would require programming languages in which to write them and operating systems to manage them.

Machine Language

One implication of the stored-program model was that programs could read and operate on other programs as data; that is, they would be capable of self-modification. Konrad Zuse had looked upon this possibility as "making a contract with the Devil" because of the potential for abuse, and he had chosen not to implement it in his machines. But self-modification was essential for achieving a true general-purpose machine.

One of the very first employments of self-modification was for computer language translation, "language" here referring to the instructions that make the machine work. Although the earliest machines worked by flipping switches, the stored-program machines were driven by stored coded instructions, and the conventions for encoding these instructions were referred to as the machine's language.

Writing programs for early computers meant using the machine's language. The form of a particular machine's language is dictated by its physical and logical structure. For example, if the machine uses registers to store intermediate results of calculations, there must be instructions for moving data between such registers.

The vocabulary and rules of syntax of machine language tend to be highly detailed and very far from the natural or mathematical language in which problems are normally formulated. The desirability of automating the translation of problems into machine language was immediately evident to users, who either had to become computer experts and programmers themselves in order to use the machines or had to rely on experts and programmers who might not fully understand the problems they were translating.

Automatic translation from pure mathematics or some other "high-level language" to machine language was therefore necessary before computers would be useful to a broader class of users. As early as the 1830s, Charles Babbage and Lady Lovelace had recognized that such translation could be done by machine, but they made no attempt to follow up on this idea and simply wrote their programs in machine language.

Howard Aiken, working in the 1930s, also saw the virtue of automated translation from a high-level language to machine language. Aiken proposed a coding machine that would be dedicated to this task, accepting high-level programs and producing the actual machine-language instructions that the computer would process.

But a separate machine was not actually necessary. The IAS model guaranteed that the stored-program computer would have the power to serve as its own coding machine. The translator program, written in machine language and running on the computer, would be fed the target program as data, and it would output machine-language instructions. This plan was altogether feasible, but the cost of the machines was so great that it was not seen as cost-effective to use them for anything that a human could do — including program translation.

Two forces, in fact, argued against the early development of high-level computer languages. One was skepticism that anyone outside the "priesthood" of computer operators could or would use computers directly. Consequently, early computer makers saw no need to make them more accessible to people who would not use them anyway. A second reason was efficiency. Any translation process would necessarily add to the computing time necessary to solve a problem, and mathematicians and operators were far cheaper by the hour than computers.

Programmers did, though, come up with specialized high-level languages, or HLLs, for computer instruction—even without automatic translators to turn their programs into machine language. They simply did the translation by hand. They did this because casting problems in an intermediate programming language, somewhere between mathematics and the highly detailed language of the machine, had the advantage of making it easier to understand the program's logical structure and to correct, or debug, any defects in the program.

The early HLLs thus were paper-and-pencil methods of recasting problems in an intermediate form that made it easier to write code for a machine. Herman Goldstine, with contributions from his wife, Adele Goldstine, and from John von Neumann, created a graphical representation of this process: flow diagrams. Although the diagrams were only a notational device, they were widely circulated and had great influence, evolving into what are known today as flowcharts.

Zuse's Plankalkül

Konrad Zuse developed the first real programming language, Plankalkül ("Plan Calculus"), in 1944–45. Zuse's language allowed for the creation of procedures (also called routines or subroutines; stored chunks of code that could be invoked repeatedly to perform routine operations such as taking a square root) and structured data (such as a record in a database, with a mixture of alphabetic and numeric data representing, for instance, name, address, and birth date). In addition, it provided conditional statements that could modify program execution, as well as repeat, or loop, statements that would cause a marked block of statements or a subroutine to be repeated a specified number of times or for as long as some condition held.

Zuse knew that computers could do more than arithmetic, but he was aware of the propensity of anyone introduced to them to view them as nothing more than calculators. So he took pains to demonstrate nonnumeric solutions with Plankalkül. He wrote programs to check the syntactical correctness of Boolean expressions (an application in logic and text handling) and even to check chess moves.

Unlike flowcharts, Zuse's program was no intermediate language intended for pencil-and-paper translation by mathematicians. It was deliberately intended for machine translation, and Zuse did some work toward implementing a translator for Plankalkül. He did not get very far, however; he had to disassemble his machine near the end of the war and was not able to put it back together and work on it for several years. Unfortunately, his language and his work, which were roughly a dozen years ahead of their time, were not generally known outside Germany.

INTERPRETERS

HLL coding was attempted right from the start of the stored-program era in the late 1940s. Shortcode, or short-order code, was the first such language actually implemented. Suggested by John Mauchly in 1949, it was implemented by William Schmitt for the BINAC computer in that year and for UNIVAC in 1950. Shortcode went through multiple steps: first it converted the alphabetic statements of the language to numeric codes, and then it translated these numeric codes into machine language. It was an interpreter, meaning that it translated HLL statements and executed, or performed, them one at a time—a slow process. Because of their slow execution, interpreters are now rarely used outside of program development, where they may help a programmer to locate errors quickly.

COMPILERS

An alternative to this approach is what is now known as compilation. In compilation, the entire HLL program is converted to machine language and stored for later execution. Although translation may take many hours or even days, once the translated program is stored, it can be recalled anytime in the form of a fast-executing machine-language program.

In 1952 Heinz Rutishauser, who had worked with Zuse on his computers after the war, wrote an influential paper, "*Automatische Rechenplanfertigung bei programmgesteuerten Rechenmaschinen*" (loosely translatable as "Computer Automated Conversion of Code to Machine Language"), in which he laid down the foundations of compiler construction and described two proposed compilers. Rutishauser was later involved in creating one of the most carefully defined programming languages of this early era, ALGOL (described below).

Then, in September 1952, Alick Glennie, a student at the University of Manchester, England, created the first of several programs called Autocode for the Manchester Mark I. Autocode was the first compiler actually to be implemented. (The language that it compiled was called by the same name.) Glennie's compiler had little influence, however. When J. Halcombe Laning created a compiler for the Whirlwind computer at MIT two years later, he met with similar lack of interest. Both compilers had the fatal drawback of producing code that ran slower (10 times slower, in the case of Laning's) than code hand-written in machine language.

GRACE MURRAY HOPPER

While the high cost of computer resources placed a premium on fast hand-coded machine-language programs, one individual worked tirelessly to promote high-level programming languages and their associated compilers. Grace Murray Hopper taught mathematics at Vassar College, Poughkeepsie, N.Y., from 1931 to 1943 before

U.S. Navy Commodore Grace Hopper. Cynthia Johnson/Time & Life Pictures/Getty Images

joining the U.S. Naval Reserve. In 1944 she was assigned to the Bureau of Ordnance Computation Project at Harvard University, where she programmed the Mark I under the direction of Howard Aiken. After World War II she joined J. Presper Eckert, Jr., and John Mauchly at their new company and, among other things, wrote compiler software for the BINAC and UNIVAC systems. Throughout the 1950s Hopper campaigned earnestly for high-level languages across the United States, and through her public appearances she helped to remove resistance to the idea. Such urging found a receptive audience at IBM, where the management wanted to add computers to the company's successful line of business machines.

IBM Develops FORTRAN

In the early 1950s John Backus convinced his managers at IBM to let him put together a team to design a language and write a compiler for it. He had a machine in mind: the IBM 704, which had built-in floating-point math operations. That the 704 used floating-point representation made it especially useful for scientific work, and Backus believed that a scientifically oriented programming language would make the machine even more attractive. Still, he understood the resistance to anything that slowed a machine down, and he set out to produce a language and a compiler that would produce code that ran virtually as fast as hand-coded machine language—and at the same time made the program-writing process a lot easier.

By 1954 Backus and a team of programmers had designed the language, which they called FORTRAN (Formula Translation). Programs written in FORTRAN looked a lot more like mathematics than machine instructions:

```
DO 10 J = 1,11
I = 11 - J
Y = F(A(I + 1))
IF (400 - Y) 4,8,8
4 PRINT 5,1
5 FORMAT (I10, 10H TOO LARGE)
```

The compiler was written, and the language was released with a professional-looking typeset manual (a first for programming languages) in 1957.

FORTRAN took another step toward making programming more accessible, allowing comments in the programs. The ability to insert annotations, marked to be ignored by the translator program but readable by a human, meant that a well-annotated program could be read in a certain sense by people with no programming knowledge at all. For the first time a nonprogrammer could get an idea what a program did—or at least what it was intended to do—by reading (part of) the code. It was an obvious but powerful step in opening up computers to a wider audience.

FORTRAN has continued to evolve, and it retains a large user base in academia and among scientists.

COBOL

About the time that Backus and his team invented FORTRAN, Hopper's group at UNIVAC released Math-matic, a FORTRAN-like language for UNIVAC computers. It was slower than FORTRAN and not particularly successful. Another language developed at Hopper's laboratory at the same time had more influence. Flow-matic used a more English-like syntax and vocabulary:

1 COMPARE PART-NUMBER (A) TO PART-
NUMBER (B);
IF GREATER GO TO OPERATION 13;
IF EQUAL GO TO OPERATION 4;
OTHERWISE GO TO OPERATION 2.

Flow-matic led to the development by Hopper's group of COBOL (Common Business-Oriented Language) in 1959. COBOL was explicitly a business programming language with a very verbose English-like style. It became central to the wide acceptance of computers by business after 1959.

ALGOL

Although both FORTRAN and COBOL were universal languages (meaning that they could, in principle, be used to solve any problem that a computer could unravel), FORTRAN was better suited for mathematicians and engineers, whereas COBOL was explicitly a business programming language.

During the late 1950s a multitude of programming languages appeared. This proliferation of incompatible specialized languages spurred an interest in the United States and Europe to create a single "second-generation" language. A transatlantic committee soon formed to determine specifications for ALGOL (Algorithmic Language), as the new language would be called. Backus, on the American side, and Heinz Rutishauser, on the European side, were among the most influential committee members.

Although ALGOL introduced some important language ideas, it was not a commercial success. Customers preferred a known specialized language, such as FORTRAN or COBOL, to an unknown general-programming language. Only Pascal, a scientific programming-language offshoot of ALGOL, survives.

OPERATING SYSTEMS

In order to make the early computers truly useful and efficient, two major innovations in software were needed. One was high-level programming languages (as described above). The other was control. Today the systemwide control functions of a computer are generally subsumed under the term *operating system*, or OS. An OS handles the behind-the-scenes activities of a computer, such as orchestrating the transitions from one program to another and managing access to disk storage and peripheral devices.

CONTROL PROGRAMS

The need for some kind of supervisor program was quickly recognized, but the design requirements for such a program were daunting. The supervisor program would have to run in parallel with an application program somehow, monitor its actions in some way, and seize control when necessary. Moreover, the essential— and difficult—feature of even a rudimentary supervisor program was the interrupt facility. It had to be able to stop a running program when necessary but save the state of the program and all registers so that after the interruption was over the program could be restarted from where it left off.

The first computer with such a true interrupt system was the UNIVAC 1103A, which had a single interrupt triggered by one fixed condition. In 1959 the Lincoln Labs TX2 generalized the interrupt capability, making it possible to set various interrupt conditions under software control. However, it would be one company, IBM, that would create, and dominate, a market for business computers. IBM established its primacy primarily through one invention: the IBM 360 operating system.

THE IBM 360

IBM had been selling business machines since early in the century and had built Howard Aiken's computer to his architectural specifications. But the company had been slow to implement the stored-program digital computer architecture of the early 1950s. It did develop the IBM 650, a (like UNIVAC) decimal implementation of the IAS plan—and the first computer to sell more than 1,000 units.

The invention of the transistor in 1947 led IBM to reengineer its early machines from electromechanical or vacuum tube to transistor technology in the late 1950s (although the UNIVAC Model 80, delivered in 1958, was the first transistor computer). These transistorized machines are commonly referred to as second-generation computers.

Two IBM inventions, the magnetic disk and the high-speed chain printer, led to an expansion of the market and to the unprecedented sale of 12,000 computers of one model: the IBM 1401. The chain printer required a lot of magnetic core memory, and IBM engineers packaged the printer support, core memory, and disk support into the 1401, one of the first computers to use this solid-state technology.

IBM had several lines of computers developed by independent groups of engineers within the company: a scientific-technical line, a commercial data-processing line, an accounting line, a decimal machine line, and a line of supercomputers. Each line had a distinct hardware-dependent operating system, and each required separate development and maintenance of its associated application software. In the early 1960s IBM began designing a machine that would take the best of all these disparate

This photo shows a vacuum tube and a transistor, functional forebearers of semiconductor chips. Time & Life Pictures/Getty Images

lines, add some new technology and new ideas, and replace all the company's computers with one single line, the 360. At an estimated development cost of $5 billion, IBM literally bet the company's future on this new, untested architecture.

The 360 was in fact an architecture, not a single machine. Designers G. M. Amdahl, F. P. Brooks, and G. A. Blaauw explicitly separated the 360 architecture from its implementation details. The 360 architecture was intended to span a wide range of machine implementations and multiple generations of machines. The first 360 models were hybrid transistor–integrated circuit machines. Integrated circuit computers are commonly referred to as third-generation computers.

Key to the architecture was the operating system. OS/360 ran on all machines built to the 360 architecture—initially six machines spanning a wide range of performance characteristics and later many more machines. It had a shielded supervisory system (unlike the 1401, which could be interfered with by application programs), and it reserved certain operations as privileged in that they could be performed only by the supervisor program.

The first IBM 360 computers were delivered in 1965. The 360 architecture represented a continental divide in the relative importance of hardware and software. After the 360, computers were defined by their operating systems.

Visitors look at a display featuring a vintage IBM 360 computer and accessories at the Computer History Museum in Mountain View, Calif. Justin Sullivan/Getty Images

The market, on the other hand, was defined by IBM. In the late 1950s and into the 1960s, it was common to refer to the computer industry as "IBM and the Seven Dwarfs," a reference to the relatively diminutive market share of its nearest rivals—Sperry Rand (UNIVAC), Control Data Corporation (CDC), Honeywell, Burroughs, General Electric (GE), RCA, and National Cash Register Co. During this time IBM had some 60–70 percent of all computer sales. The 360 did nothing to lessen the giant's dominance. When the market did open up somewhat, it was not due to the efforts of, nor was it in favour of, the dwarfs. Yet, while "IBM and the Seven Dwarfs" (soon reduced to "IBM and the BUNCH of Five," BUNCH being an acronym for Burroughs, UNIVAC, NCR, CDC, and Honeywell) continued to build Big Iron, a fundamental change was taking place in how computers were accessed.

BIG BLUE: IBM RULES

Incorporated in 1911 as the Computing-Tabulating-Recording Company, IBM assumed its present name in 1924 under the leadership of Thomas Watson, a man of considerable marketing skill. Watson built the then-floundering company into the leading American manufacturer of punch-card tabulating systems used by governments and private businesses. He also developed a highly disciplined and competitive sales force that adapted the company's custom-built tabulating systems to the needs of particular customers.

During World War II, IBM helped construct several high-speed electromechanical calculators that were the precursors of electronic computers. But the firm refrained from producing these electronic data-processing systems until Watson's son, Thomas Watson, Jr., became president of the company in 1952 and sponsored an all-out push into that field. Having entered the computer field, IBM's size allowed it to invest heavily in development. This investment capability, added to its dominance in office-calculating machines, its marketing expertise, and its commitment to repair and service its own equipment, allowed IBM quickly to assume the predominant position in the American computer market. By the 1960s it was producing 70 percent of the world's computers and 80 percent of those used in the United States.

IBM's specialty was mainframe computers—i.e., expensive medium- to large-scale computers that could process numerical data at great speeds. The company did not enter the growing market for personal computers until 1981, when it introduced the IBM Personal Computer. This product achieved a major share of the market, but IBM was nevertheless unable to exercise its accustomed dominance as a maker of personal computers. New semiconductor chip–based technologies were making computers smaller and easier to manufacture, allowing smaller companies to enter the field and exploit new developments such as workstations, computer networks, and computer graphics. IBM's enormous size hindered it from responding rapidly to these accelerating rates of technological change, and by the 1990s the company had downsized considerably.

In 2002 IBM sold its magnetic hard drive business and by 2005 had stopped building a device that it had invented in 1956. In December 2005 IBM sold its personal computer division to the Lenovo Group, a major Chinese manufacturer. With these divestitures, IBM shifted away from manufacturing so-called commodity products in order to concentrate on its computer services, software, supercomputer, and scientific research divisions. IBM consistently places one of its supercomputers at or near the top of the industry's list of most powerful machines. The company holds more than 40,000 active patents worldwide, which generate considerable income from royalties.

TIME-SHARING FROM PROJECT MAC TO UNIX

In 1959 Christopher Strachey in the United Kingdom and John McCarthy in the United States independently described something they called time-sharing. Meanwhile, computer pioneer J. C. R. Licklider at

MIT began to promote the idea of interactive computing as an alternative to batch processing. Batch processing was the normal mode of operating computers at the time: a user handed a deck of punched cards to an operator, who fed them to the machine, and an hour or more later the printed output would be made available for pickup. Licklider's wnotion of interactive programming involved typing on a teletype or other keyboard and getting more or less immediate feedback from the computer on the teletype's printer mechanism or some other output device. This was how the Whirlwind computer had been operated at MIT in 1950, and it was essentially what Strachey and McCarthy had in mind at the end of the decade.

By November 1961 a prototype time-sharing system had been produced and tested. It was built by Fernando Corbato and Robert Jano at MIT, and it connected an IBM 709 computer with three users typing away at IBM Flexowriters. This was only a prototype for a more elaborate time-sharing system that Corbato was working on, called Compatible Time-Sharing System, or CTSS. Still, Corbato was waiting for the appropriate technology to build that system. It was clear that electromechanical and vacuum tube technologies would not be adequate for the computational demands that time-sharing would place on the machines. Fast, transistor-based computers were needed.

In the meantime, Licklider had been placed in charge of a U.S. government program called the Advanced Research Projects Agency (ARPA), created in response to the launch of the *Sputnik* satellite by the Soviet Union in 1957. ARPA researched interesting technological areas, and under Licklider's leadership it focused on time-sharing and interactive computing. With ARPA support, CTSS evolved into Project MAC, which went online in 1963.

Project MAC was only the beginning. Other similar time-sharing projects followed rapidly at various research institutions, and some commercial products began to be released that also were called interactive or time-sharing. Time-sharing represented a different interaction model, and it needed a new programming language to support it. Researchers created several such languages, most notably BASIC (Beginner's All-Purpose Symbolic Instruction Code), which was invented in 1964 at Dartmouth College, Hanover, N.H., by John Kemeny and Thomas Kurtz. BASIC had features that made it ideal for time-sharing, and it was easy enough to be used by its target audience: college students. Kemeny and Kurtz wanted to open computers to a broader group of users and deliberately designed BASIC with that goal in mind. They succeeded.

Time-sharing also called for a new kind of operating system. Researchers at AT&T (American Telephone and Telegraph Company) and GE tackled the problem with funding from ARPA via Project MAC and an ambitious plan to implement time-sharing on a new computer with a new time-sharing-oriented operating system. AT&T dropped out after the project was well under way, but GE went ahead, and the result was the Multics operating system running on the GE 645 computer. GE 645 exemplified the time-shared computer in 1965, and Multics was the model of a time-sharing operating system, built to be up seven days a week, 24 hours a day.

When AT&T dropped out of the project and removed the GE machines from its laboratories, researchers at AT&T's high-tech research arm, Bell Laboratories, were upset. They felt they needed the time-sharing capabilities of Multics for their work, and so two Bell Labs workers, Ken Thompson and Dennis Ritchie, wrote their own operating system. Since the operating system was inspired by Multics but would initially be somewhat simpler, they called it UNIX.

UNIX embodied, among other innovations, the notion of pipes. Pipes allowed a user to pass the results of one program to another program for use as input. This led to a style of programming in which small, targeted, single-function programs were joined together to achieve a more complicated goal. Perhaps the most influential aspect of UNIX, though, was that Bell Labs distributed the source code (the uncompiled, human-readable form of the code that made up the operating system) freely to colleges and universities—but made no offer to support it. The freely distributed source code led to a rapid, and somewhat divergent, evolution of UNIX. Whereas initial support was attracted by its free availability, its robust multitasking and well-developed network security features have continued to make it the most common operating system for academic institutions and World Wide Web servers.

MINICOMPUTERS

About 1965, roughly coterminous with the development of time-sharing, a new kind of computer came on the scene. Small and relatively inexpensive (typically onc-tenth the cost of the Big Iron machines), the new machines were stored-program computers with all the generality of the computers then in use but stripped down. The new machines were called minicomputers. (About the same time, the larger traditional computers began to be called mainframes.) Minicomputers were designed for easy connection to scientific instruments and other input/output devices, had a simplified architecture, were implemented using fast transistors, and were typically programmed in assembly language with little support for high-level languages.

Other small, inexpensive computing devices were available at the time but were not considered minicomputers. These were special-purpose scientific machines or small character-based or decimal-based machines such as the IBM 1401. They were not considered "minis," however, because they did not meet the needs of the initial market for minis—that is, for a lab computer to control instruments and collect and analyze data.

The market for minicomputers evolved over time, but it was scientific laboratories that created the category. It was an essentially untapped market, and those manufacturers who established an early foothold dominated it. Only one of the mainframe manufacturers, Honeywell, was able to break into the minicomputer market in any significant way. The other main minicomputer players, such as Digital Equipment Corporation (DEC), Data General Corporation, Hewlett-Packard Company, and Texas Instruments Incorporated, all came from fields outside mainframe computing, frequently from the field of electronic test equipment. The failure of the mainframe companies to gain a foothold in the minimarket may have stemmed from their failure to recognize that minis were distinct in important ways from the small computers that these companies were already making.

The first minicomputer, although it was not recognized as such at the time, may have been the MIT Whirlwind in 1950. It was designed for instrument control and had many, although not all, of the features of later minis. DEC, founded in 1957 by Kenneth Olsen and Harlan Anderson, produced one of the first minicomputers, the Programmed Data Processor, or PDP-1, in 1959. At a price of $120,000, the PDP-1 sold for a fraction of the cost of mainframe computers, albeit with vastly more limited capabilities. But it was the PDP-8, using the recently invented integrated circuit (a set of interconnected transistors and resistors on a single silicon wafer, or chip) and selling for around $20,000 (falling to $3,000 by the late 1970s), that was the first true mass-market minicomputer. The PDP-8 was released in 1965, the same year as the first IBM 360 machines.

The PDP-8 was the prototypical mini. It was designed to be programmed in assembly language; it was easy—physically, logically, and electrically—to attach a wide variety of input/output devices and scientific instruments to it; and it was architecturally stripped down with little support for programming—it even lacked multiplication and division operations in its initial release. It had a mere 4,096 words of memory, and its word length was 12 bits—very short even by the standards of the times. (The word is the smallest chunk of memory that a program can refer to independently; the size of the word limits the complexity of the instruction set and the efficiency of mathematical operations.) The PDP-8's short word and small memory made it relatively underpowered for the time, but its low price more than compensated for this.

The PDP-11 shipped five years later, relaxing some of the constraints imposed on the PDP-8. It was designed to support high-level languages, had more memory and more power generally, was produced in 10 different models over 10 years, and was a great success. It was followed

The PDP-8, or Straight-8, minicomputer was manufactured by the Digital Equipment Corporation (DEC), United States. It is shown here with the casing removed. SSPL via Getty Images

by the VAX line, which supported an advanced operating system called VAX/VMS—VMS standing for virtual memory system, an innovation that effectively expanded the memory of the machine by allowing disk or other peripheral storage to serve as extra memory. By this time (the early 1970s) DEC was vying with Sperry Rand (manufacturer of the UNIVAC computer) for position as the second largest computer company in the world, though it was producing machines that had little in common with the original prototypical minis.

Although the minis' early growth was due to their use as scientific instrument controllers and data loggers, their compelling feature turned out to be their approachability. After years of standing in line to use departmental, universitywide, or companywide machines through intermediaries, scientists and researchers could now buy their own computer and run it themselves in their own laboratories. And they had intimate access to the internals of the machine, the stripped-down architecture making it possible for a smart graduate student to reconfigure the machine to do something not intended by the manufacturer. With their own computers in their labs, researchers began to use minis for all sorts of new purposes, and the manufacturers adapted later releases of the machines to the evolving demands of the market.

The minicomputer revolution lasted about a decade. By 1975 it was coming to a close, but not because minis were becoming less attractive. The mini was about to be eclipsed by another technology: the new integrated circuits, which would soon be used to build the smallest, most affordable computer to date—the personal computer.

CHAPTER 4
THE PERSONAL COMPUTER REVOLUTION

Before 1970, computers were big machines requiring thousands of separate transistors. They were operated by specialized technicians, who often dressed in white lab coats and were commonly referred to as a computer priesthood. The machines were expensive and difficult to use. Few people came in direct contact with them, not even their programmers. The typical interaction was as follows: a programmer coded instructions and data on preformatted paper, a keypunch operator transferred the data onto punch cards, a computer operator fed the cards into a card reader, and the computer executed the instructions or stored the cards' information for later processing. Advanced installations might allow users limited interaction with the computer more directly, but still remotely, via time-sharing through the use of cathode-ray tube terminals or teletype machines.

There were essentially two types of computers. First there were the room-sized mainframes, costing hundreds of thousands of dollars, that were built one at a time by companies such as IBM and CDC. Then there were the smaller, cheaper, mass-produced minicomputers, costing tens of thousands of dollars, that were built by a handful of companies, such as Digital Equipment Corporation and Hewlett-Packard Company, for scientific laboratories and businesses. Most people had no direct contact with either type, and the machines were popularly viewed as impersonal giant brains that threatened to eliminate jobs through automation. The idea that anyone would have his or her own desktop computer was generally regarded as far-fetched. Nevertheless, with advances in integrated circuit technology, the necessary building blocks for desktop computing began to emerge in the early 1970s.

THE MICROPROCESSOR

One of the most elementary building blocks was the microprocessor, an extremely complicated integrated circuit composed of millions of transistors that contains the arithmetic, logic, and control circuitry necessary to perform the functions of a digital computer's central processing unit. The device was made possible by the invention of the solid-state transistor.

INTEGRATED CIRCUITS

William Shockley, a co-inventor of the transistor, started Shockley Semiconductor Laboratories in 1955 in his hometown of Palo Alto, Calif. In 1957 his eight top researchers left to form Fairchild Semiconductor Corporation, funded by Fairchild Camera and Instrument Corporation. Along with Hewlett-Packard, another Palo Alto firm, Fairchild Semiconductor was the seed of what would become known as Silicon Valley. Historically, Fairchild will always deserve recognition as one of the most important semiconductor companies, having served as the training ground for most of the entrepreneurs who went on to start their own computer companies in the 1960s and early 1970s.

From the mid-1960s into the early '70s, Fairchild Semiconductor Corporation and Texas Instruments Incorporated were the leading manufacturers of integrated circuits (ICs) and were continually increasing the number of electronic components embedded in a single silicon wafer, or chip. As the number of components escalated into the thousands, these chips began to be referred to as large-scale integration chips, and computers using them are sometimes called fourth-generation computers. The invention of the microprocessor was the culmination of this trend.

Although computers were still rare and often regarded as a threat to employment, calculators were common and accepted in offices. With advances in semiconductor technology, a market was emerging for sophisticated electronic desktop calculators. It was, in fact, a calculator project that turned into a milestone in the history of computer technology.

THE INTEL 4004

In 1969 Busicom, a Japanese calculator company, commissioned Intel Corporation to make the chips for a line of calculators that Busicom intended to sell. Custom chips were made for many clients, and this was one more such contract, hardly unusual at the time.

Intel was one of several semiconductor companies to emerge in Silicon Valley, having spun off from Fairchild Semiconductor. Intel's president, Robert Noyce, while at Fairchild, had invented planar integrated circuits, a process in which the wiring was directly embedded in the silicon along with the electronic components at the manufacturing stage.

Intel had planned on focusing its business on memory chips, but Busicom's request for custom chips for a calculator turned out to be a most valuable diversion. While specialized chips were effective at their given task, their small market made them expensive. Three Intel engineers—Federico Faggin, Marcian ("Ted") Hoff, and Stan Mazor—considered the request of the Japanese firm and proposed a more versatile design.

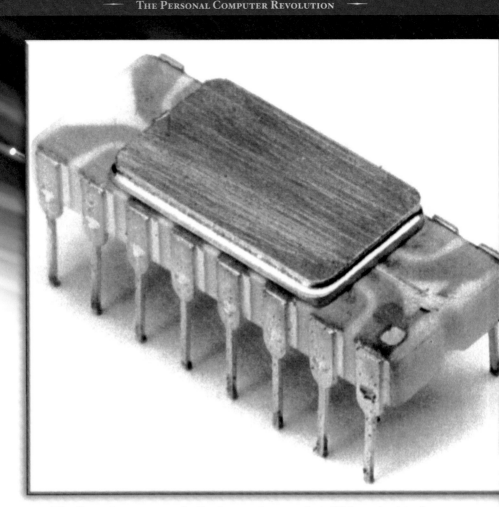

The first microprocessor, the Intel 4004, in 1971. Apic/Hulton Archive/ Getty Images

Hoff had experience with minicomputers, which could do anything the calculator could do and more. He rebelled at building a special purpose device when the technology existed to build a general-purpose one. The general-purpose device he had in mind, however, would be a lot like a computer, and at that time computers intimidated people while calculators did not. Moreover, there was a clear and large market for calculators and a limited one for computers—and, after all, the customer had commissioned a calculator chip.

Nevertheless, Hoff prevailed, and Intel proposed a design that was functionally very similar to a minicomputer (although not in size, power, attachable physical devices such as printers, or many other practical ways). In addition to performing the input/output functions that most ICs carried out, the design would form the instructions for the IC and would help to control, send, and receive signals from other chips and devices. A set of instructions was stored in memory, and the chip could read them and respond to them. The device would thus do everything that Busicom wanted, but it would do a lot more: it was the essence of a general-purpose computer. There was little obvious demand for such a device, but the Intel team, understanding the drawbacks of special-purpose ICs, sensed that it was an economical device that would, somehow, find a market.

At first Busicom was not interested, but Intel decided to go forward with the design anyway, and the Japanese company eventually accepted it. Intel named the chip the 4004, which referred to the number of features and transistors it had. These included memory, input/output, control, and arithmetical/logical capacities. It came to be called a microprocessor or microcomputer. It is this chip that is referred to as the brain of the personal desktop computer—the central processing unit, or CPU.

Busicom eventually sold over 100,000 calculators powered by the 4004. Busicom later also accepted a one-time payment of $60,000 that gave Intel exclusive rights to the 4004 design, and Intel began marketing the chip to other manufacturers in 1971.

The 4004 had significant limitations. As a four-bit processor, it was capable of only 2^4, or 16, distinct combinations, or "words." To distinguish the 26 letters of the alphabet and up to six punctuation symbols, the computer had to combine two four-bit words. Nevertheless, the 4004 achieved a level of fame when Intel found a high-profile customer for it: it was used on the *Pioneer 10* space probe, launched on March 2, 1972.

It became a little easier to see the potential of microprocessors when Intel introduced an eight-bit processor, the 8008, in November 1972. (In 1974 the 8008 was reengineered with a larger, more versatile instruction set as the 8080.) In 1972 Intel was still a small company, albeit with two new and revolutionary products. But no one—certainly not their inventors—had figured out exactly what to do with Intel's microprocessors.

Intel placed in electronics magazines articles expounding the microprocessors' capabilities and proselytized engineering organizations and companies in the hope that others would come up with applications. With the basic capabilities of a computer now available on a tiny speck of silicon, some observers realized that this was the dawn of a new age of computing. That new age would centre on the microcomputer.

THE MICROCOMPUTER

Though the young engineering executives at Intel could sense the ground shifting upon the introduction of their new microprocessors, the leading computer manufacturers did not. It should not have taken a visionary to observe the trend of cheaper, faster, and more powerful devices. Nevertheless, even after the invention of the microprocessor, few could imagine a market for personal computers.

The advent of the microprocessor did not inspire IBM or any other large company to begin producing personal computers. Time after time, the big computer companies overlooked the opportunity to bring computing capabilities to a much broader market. In some cases, they turned down explicit proposals by their own engineers to build such machines. Instead, the new generation of microcomputers emerged from the minds and passions of electronics hobbyists and entrepreneurs.

EARLY COMPUTER ENTHUSIASTS

In the San Francisco Bay area, the advances of the semiconductor industry were gaining recognition and stimulating a grassroots computer movement. Lee Felsenstein, an electronics engineer active in the student antiwar movement of the 1960s, started an organization called Community Memory to install computer terminals in storefronts. This movement was a sign of the times, an attempt by computer cognoscenti to empower the masses by giving ordinary individuals access to a public computer network.

The frustration felt by engineers and electronics hobbyists who wanted easier access to computers was expressed in articles in the electronics magazines in the early 1970s. Magazines such as *Popular Electronics* and *Radio Electronics* helped spread the notion of a personal computer. And in the San Francisco Bay area and elsewhere hobbyists organized computer clubs to discuss how to build their own computers.

Dennis Allison wrote a version of BASIC for these early personal computers and, with Bob Albrecht, published the code in 1975 in a newsletter called *Dr. Dobb's Journal of Computer Calisthenics and Orthodontia*, later changed to *Dr. Dobb's Journal*. For more than 30 years *Dr. Dobb's* continued to publish programming tips and public domain software, making programs available to anyone willing to type them into a computer and reflecting the early passion for sharing computer knowledge and software.

THE ALTAIR

In September 1973 *Radio Electronics* published an article describing a "TV Typewriter," which was a computer terminal that could connect a hobbyist with a mainframe computer. It was written by Don Lancaster, an aerospace engineer and fire spotter in Arizona who was also a prolific author of do it yourself articles for electronics hobbyists. The TV Typewriter provided the first display of alphanumeric information on a common television set. It influenced a generation of computer hobbyists to start thinking about real "home-brewed" computers.

The next step was the personal computer itself. That same year a French company, R2E, developed the Micral microcomputer using the 8008 processor. The Micral was the first commercial, non-kit microcomputer. Although the company sold 500 Micrals in France that year, it was little known among American hobbyists.

Instead, a company called Micro Instrumentation Telemetry Systems, which rapidly became known as MITS, made the big American splash. This company, located in a tiny office in an Albuquerque, N.M., shopping centre, had started out selling radio transmitters for model airplanes in 1968. It expanded into the kit calculator business in the early 1970s. This move was terribly ill-timed because other, larger manufacturers such as Hewlett-Packard and Texas Instruments (itself a leading designer of ICs) soon moved into the market with mass-produced calculators. As a result, calculators quickly became smaller, more powerful, and cheaper. By 1974 the average cost for a calculator had dropped from several hundred dollars to about $25, and MITS was on the verge of bankruptcy.

In need of a new product, MITS came up with the idea of selling a computer kit. The kit, containing all of the components necessary to build an Altair computer, sold

The Altair. SSPL via Getty Images

for $397, barely more than the list cost of the Intel 8080 microprocessor that it used. A January 1975 cover article in *Popular Electronics* generated hundreds of orders for the kit, and MITS was saved.

The firm did its best to live up to its promise of delivery within 60 days, and to do so it limited manufacture to a bare-bones kit that included a box, a CPU board with 256 bytes of memory, and a front panel. The machines, especially the early ones, had only limited reliability. To make them work required many hours of assembly by an electronics expert.

When assembled, Altairs were blue, box-shaped machines that measured 17 inches by 18 inches by 7 inches (approximately 43 cm by 46 cm by 18 cm). There was no keyboard, video terminal, paper-tape reader, or printer. There was no software. All programming was in assembly language. The only way to input programs was by setting switches on the front panel for each instruction, step-by-step. A pattern of flashing lights on the front panel indicated the results of a program.

Just getting the Altair to blink its lights represented an accomplishment. Nevertheless, it sparked people's interest. In Silicon Valley, members of a nascent hobbyist group called the Homebrew Computer Club gathered around an Altair at one of their first meetings. Homebrew epitomized the passion and antiestablishment camaraderie that characterized the hobbyist community in Silicon Valley. At their meetings, chaired by Felsenstein, attendees compared digital devices that they were constructing and discussed the latest articles in electronics magazines.

In one important way, MITS modeled the Altair after the minicomputer. It had a bus structure, a data path for sending instructions throughout its circuitry that would allow it to house and communicate with add-on circuit boards. The Altair hardly represented a singular revolutionary invention, along the lines of the transistor, but it did encourage sweeping change, giving hobbyists the confidence to take the next step.

THE HOBBY MARKET EXPANDS

Some entrepreneurs, particularly in the San Francisco Bay area, saw opportunities to build add-on devices, or peripherals, for the Altair; others decided to design competitive hardware products. Because different machines might use different data paths, or buses, peripherals built for one computer might not work with another computer. This led the emerging industry to petition the Institute for Electrical and Electronics Engineers to select a standard bus. The resulting standard, the S-100 bus, was open for all to use and became ubiquitous among early personal computers. Standardizing on a common bus helped to expand the market for early peripheral manufacturers, spurred the development of new devices, and relieved computer manufacturers of the onerous need to develop their own proprietary peripherals.

These early microcomputer companies took the first steps toward building a personal computer industry, but most of them eventually collapsed, unable to build enough reliable machines or to offer sufficient customer support. In general, most of the early companies lacked the proper balance of engineers, entrepreneurs, capital, and marketing experience. But perhaps even more significant was a dearth of software that could make microcomputers useful to a larger, nonhobbyist market.

EARLY MICROCOMPUTER SOFTWARE: FROM *Star Trek* TO MICROSOFT

The first programs developed for the hobbyists' microcomputers were games. With the early machines limited in graphic capabilities, most of these were text-based adventure or role-playing games. However, there were a few graphical games, such as *Star Trek*, which were popular on mainframes and minicomputers and were converted to run on microcomputers. One company created the game *Micro Chess* and used the profits to fund the development of an important program called VisiCalc, the industry's first spreadsheet software. These games, in addition to demonstrating some of the microcomputer's capabilities, helped to convince ordinary individuals, in particular small-business owners, that they could operate a computer.

As was the case with large computers, the creation of application software for the machines waited for the development of programming languages and operating systems. Gary Kildall developed the first operating system for a microcomputer as part of a project he contracted with Intel several years before the release of the Altair. Kildall realized that a computer had to be able to handle storage devices such as disk drives, and for this purpose he developed an operating system called CP/M.

There was no obvious use for such software at the time, and Intel agreed that Kildall could keep it. Later, when a few microcomputer companies had emerged from among the hobbyists and entrepreneurs inspired by MITS, a company called IMSAI realized that an operating system would attract more software to its machine, and it chose CP/M. Most companies followed suit, and Kildall's company, Digital Research, became one of the first software giants in the emerging microcomputer industry.

High-level languages were also needed in order for programmers to develop applications. Two young programmers realized this almost immediately upon hearing of the MITS Altair. Childhood friends William ("Bill") Gates and Paul Allen were whiz kids with computers as they grew up in Seattle, debugging software on minicomputers

In 1987, Microsoft chairman Bill Gates, behind a pile of books, holds up Bookshelf, a compact disc for computers that could contain all the information contained in the books pictured. Doug Wilson/Time & Life Pictures/ Getty Images

at the ages of 13 and 15, respectively. As teenagers they had started a company and had built the hardware and written the software that would provide statistics on traffic flow from a rubber tube strung across a highway. Later, when the Altair came out, Allen quit his job, and Gates left Harvard University, where he was a student, in order to create a version of the programming language BASIC that could run on the new computer. They licensed their version of BASIC to MITS and started calling their partnership Microsoft. The Microsoft Corporation went on to develop versions of BASIC for nearly every computer that was released. It also developed other high-level languages. When IBM eventually decided to enter the microcomputer business in 1980, it called on Microsoft for both a programming language and an operating system, and the small partnership was on its way to becoming the largest software company in the world.

APPLICATION SOFTWARE

The availability of BASIC and CP/M enabled more widespread software development. By 1977 a two-person firm called Structured Systems Group started developing a General Ledger program, perhaps the first serious business software, which sold for $995. The company shipped its software in ziplock bags with a manual, a practice that became common in the industry. General Ledger began to familiarize business managers with microcomputers. Another important program was the first microcomputer word processor, called Electric Pencil, developed by a former camera operator turned computer hobbyist. Electric Pencil was one of the first programs that allowed nontechnical people to perform useful tasks on personal computers. Nevertheless, the early personal computer companies still underestimated the value of software, and many refused to pay the software developer to convert Electric Pencil to run on their machines. Eventually the availability of some software would play a major role in determining the success of a computer.

In 1979 a Harvard business graduate named Dan Bricklin and a programmer named Bob Frankston developed VisiCalc, the first personal computer financial analysis tool. VisiCalc made business forecasting much simpler, allowing individuals to ask "What if" questions about numerical data and get the sort of immediate response that was not even possible for giant corporations using mainframe computer systems. Personal Software, the company that distributed VisiCalc, became hugely successful. With a few companies such as Microsoft leading the way, a software industry separate from the hardware field began to emerge.

THE PERSONAL COMPUTER

The transition from the microcomputers of hobbyists and engineers to true personal computers finally came in the late 1970s and 1980s, when designers, entrepreneurs, and established computer manufacturers finally understood that commercial success would come only if microcomputers could be operated by the noninitiated and could be programmed to perform useful business and personal functions. In this new type of microcomputer, software and design were as important as memory and processor speed.

COMMODORE AND TANDY ENTER THE FIELD

In late 1976 Commodore Business Machines, an established electronics firm that had been active in producing electronic calculators, bought a small hobby-computer company named MOS Technology. For the first time, an established company with extensive distribution channels would be selling a microcomputer.

The next year, another established company entered the microcomputer market. Tandy Corporation, best known for its chain of RadioShack stores, had followed the development of MITS and decided to enter the market with its own TRS-80 microcomputer, which came with four kilobytes of memory, a Z80 microprocessor, a BASIC programming language, and cassettes for data storage. To cut costs, the machine was built without the ability to type lowercase letters. Thanks to Tandy's chain of stores and the breakthrough price ($399 fully assembled and tested), the machine was successful enough to convince the company to introduce a more powerful computer two years later, the TRS-80 Model II, which could reasonably be marketed as a small-business computer. Tandy started selling its computers in greater volumes than most of the microcomputer start-ups, except for one.

APPLE INC.

Like the founding of the early chip companies and the invention of the microprocessor, the story of Apple is a key part of Silicon Valley folklore. Two whiz kids, Stephen G. Wozniak and Steven P. Jobs, shared an interest in electronics. Wozniak was an early and regular participant at Homebrew Computer Club meetings, which Jobs also occasionally attended.

Wozniak purchased one of the early microprocessors, the Mostek 6502 (made by MOS Technology), and used it to design a computer. When Hewlett-Packard, where he had an internship, declined to build his design, he shared his progress at a Homebrew meeting, where Jobs suggested that they could sell it together. Their initial plans were modest. Jobs figured that they could sell it for $50, twice what the parts cost them, and that they could sell hundreds of them to hobbyists. The product was actually only a printed circuit board. It lacked a case, a keyboard, and a power supply. Jobs got an order for 50 of the machines from Paul Terrell, owner of one of the industry's first computer retail stores and a frequent Homebrew attendee. To raise the capital to buy the parts they needed, Jobs sold his minibus and Wozniak his calculator. They met their 30-day deadline and continued production in Jobs's parents' garage.

After their initial success, Jobs sought out the kind of help that other industry pioneers had shunned. While he and Wozniak began work on the Apple II, he consulted with a venture capitalist and enlisted an advertising company to aid him in marketing. As a result, in late 1976 A. C. ("Mike") Markkula, a retired semiconductor company executive, helped write a business plan for Apple, lined up credit from a bank, and hired a serious businessman to run the venture. Apple was clearly taking a different path from its competitors. For instance, while Altair and the other microcomputer start-ups ran advertisements in technical journals, Apple ran an early colour ad in *Playboy* magazine. Its executive team lined up nationwide distributors. Apple made sure each of its subsequent products featured an elegant, consumer-style design. It also published well-written and carefully designed manuals to instruct consumers on the use of the machines. Other manuals explained all the technical details any third-party hardware or software company would have to know to build peripherals. In addition, Apple quickly built well-engineered products that made the Apple II far more useful: a printer card, a serial card, a communications card, a memory card, and a floppy disk. This distinctive approach resonated well in the marketplace.

In 1980 the Apple III was introduced. For this new computer Apple designed a new operating system, though it also offered a capability known as emulation that allowed

Cofounder of Apple Steve Jobs leans on the Macintosh 128K, the original Macintosh personal computer, featuring MacPaint, circa 1984. Bernard Gotfryd/Premium Archive/Getty Images

the machine to run the same software, albeit much slower, as the Apple II. After several months on the market the Apple III was recalled so that certain defects could be repaired (proving that Apple was not immune to the technical failures from which most early firms suffered), but upon reintroduction to the marketplace it never achieved the success of its predecessor (demonstrating how difficult it can be for a company to introduce a computer that is not completely compatible with its existing product line).

Nevertheless, the flagship Apple II and successors in that line—the Apple II+, the Apple IIe, and the Apple IIc—made Apple the leading personal computer company in the world. In 1980 it announced its first public stock offering, and its young founders became instant millionaires. After three years in business, Apple's revenues had increased from $7.8 million to $117.9 million.

INSANELY GREAT: THE MACINTOSH

In 1979 Apple cofounder Steve Jobs led a team of engineers to see the innovations created at the Xerox Corporation's Palo Alto Research Center. There they were shown the first functional graphical user interface (GUI), featuring on-screen windows, a pointing device known as a mouse, and the use of icons, or pictures, to replace the awkward protocols required by all other computers. Apple immediately incorporated these ideas into two new computers: Lisa, released in 1983, and the lower-cost Macintosh, released in 1984. Jobs himself took over the latter project, insisting that the Macintosh should be not merely great but "insanely great." The result was a revelation—perfectly in tune with the unconventional, science-fiction-esque television commercial that introduced the Macintosh during the broadcast of the 1984 Super Bowl—a $2,500 computer unlike any that preceded it.

Despite an ecstatic reaction from the media, the Macintosh initially sold below Apple's expectations. Critics noted that the Mac, as it came to be known, had insufficient memory and storage and lacked standard amenities such as cursor keys and a colour display. (Many skeptics also doubted that adults would ever want to use a machine that relied on the GUI, condemning it as "toylike" and wasteful of computational resources.) In the wake of the poor sales performance, Jobs was ousted from the company in September 1985 by its chief executive officer, John Sculley. Under Sculley, Apple steadily improved the machine. However, what really saved the Mac in those early years was Apple's 1985 introduction of an affordable laser printer along with Aldus Corporation's PageMaker, the Mac's first "killer app." Together these two innovations launched the desktop publishing revolution. Suddenly, small businesses and print shops could produce professional-looking brochures, pamphlets, and letters without having to resort to expensive lithographic processes. The graphic arts and publishing industries quickly became the Mac's single most important market. As the Mac's popularity expanded, so did Apple's fortunes, although by the mid-1990s the company had begun to flounder. In 1997 Jobs returned to head Apple again, faced with the task of replicating the Mac's success.

The Graphical User Interface

In 1982 Apple introduced its Lisa computer, a much more powerful computer with many innovations. The Lisa used a more advanced microprocessor, the Motorola 68000. It also had a different way of interacting with the user, called a graphical user interface (GUI). The GUI replaced the typed command lines common on previous computers with graphical icons on the screen that invoked actions when pointed to by a handheld pointing device called the mouse. The Lisa was not successful, but Apple was already preparing a scaled-down, lower-cost version called the Macintosh. Introduced in 1984, the Macintosh became wildly successful and, by making desktop computers easier to use, further popularized personal computers.

The Lisa and the Macintosh popularized several ideas that originated at other research laboratories in Silicon Valley and elsewhere. These underlying intellectual ideas, centered on the potential impact that computers could have on people, had been nurtured first by Vannevar Bush in the 1940s and then by Douglas Engelbart. Like Bush, who inspired him, Engelbart was a visionary. As early as 1963 he was predicting that the computer would eventually become a tool to augment human intellect, and he specifically described many of the uses computers would

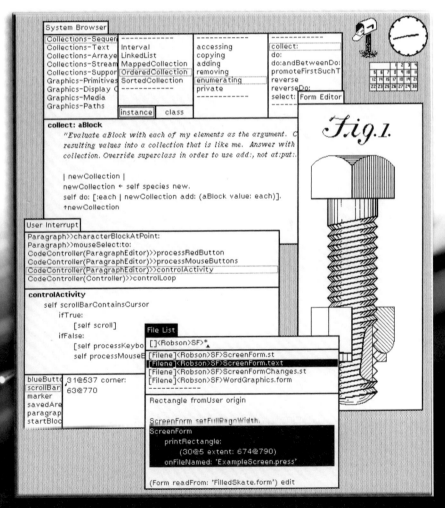

The first graphical user interface. The Xerox Alto was the first computer to use graphical icons and a mouse to control the system. Courtesy of Xerox

have, such as word processing. In 1968, as a researcher at the Stanford Research Institute (SRI), Engelbart gave a remarkable demonstration of the "NLS" (oNLine System), which featured a keyboard and a mouse, a device he had invented that was used to select commands from a menu of choices shown on a display screen. The screen was divided into multiple windows, each able to display text— a single line or an entire document—or an image. Today almost every popular computer comes with a mouse and features a system that utilizes windows on the display.

In the 1970s some of Engelbart's colleagues left SRI for Xerox Corporation's Palo Alto (Calif.) Research Center

The first computer mouse. Douglas Engelbart invented the computer mouse in 1963–64 as part of an experiment to find a better way to point and click on a display screen. Fashioned at the Stanford Research Institute, it had a carved wood casing and just one button. A subsequent model had three buttons, and Engelbart would have provided more if there had been room for more than the three microswitches to which the buttons were connected. Courtesy of the Bootstrap Institute

(PARC), which became a hotbed of computer research. In the coming years scientists at PARC pioneered many new technologies. Xerox built a prototype computer with a GUI operating system called the Alto and eventually introduced a commercial version called the Xerox Star in 1981. Xerox's efforts to market this computer were a failure, and the company withdrew from the market. Apple with its Lisa and Macintosh computers and then Microsoft with its Windows operating system imitated the design of the Alto and Star systems in many ways.

Two computer scientists at PARC, Alan Kay and Adele Goldberg, published a paper in the early 1970s describing a vision of a powerful and portable computer they dubbed the Dynabook. The prototypes of this machine were expensive and resembled sewing machines, but the vision of the two researchers greatly influenced the evolution of products that today are dubbed notebook or laptop computers.

Another researcher at PARC, Robert Metcalfe, developed a network system in 1973 that could transmit and receive data at three million bits a second, much faster than was generally thought possible at the time. Xerox did not see this as related to its core business of copiers, and it allowed Metcalfe to start his own company based on the system, called Ethernet. Ethernet eventually became the technical standard for connecting digital computers together in an office environment.

PARC researchers used Ethernet to connect their Altos together and to share another invention of theirs, the laser printer. Laser printers work by shooting a stream of light that gives a charge to the surface of a rotating drum. The charged area attracts toner powder so that when paper rolls over it an image is transferred. PARC programmers also developed numerous other innovations, such as the Smalltalk programming language, designed to make programming accessible to users who were not computer experts, and a text editor called Bravo, which displayed text on a computer screen exactly as it would look on paper.

Xerox PARC came up with these innovations but left it to others to commercialize them. Today they are viewed as commonplace.

THE IBM PERSONAL COMPUTER

The entry of IBM did more to legitimize personal computers than any event in the industry's history. By 1980 the personal computer field was starting to interest the large computer companies. Hewlett-Packard, which had earlier turned down Stephen G. Wozniak's proposal to enter the personal computer field, was now ready to enter this business, and in January 1980 it brought out its HP-85. Hewlett-Packard's machine was more expensive ($3,250) than those of most competitors, and it used a cassette tape drive for storage while most companies were already using disk drives. Another problem was its closed architecture, which made it difficult for third parties to develop applications or software for it.

Throughout its history IBM had shown a willingness to place bets on new technologies, such as the 360 architecture. Its long-term success was due largely to its ability to innovate and to adapt its business to technological change. "Big Blue," as the company was commonly known, introduced the first computer disk storage system, the RAMAC, which showed off its capabilities by answering world history questions in 10 languages at the 1958 World's Fair. From 1956 to 1971 IBM sales had grown from $900 million to $8 billion, and its number of employees had increased from 72,500 to 270,000. IBM had also innovated new marketing techniques such as the unbundling of hardware, software, and computer services. So it was not a surprise that IBM would enter the fledgling but promising personal computer business.

In fact, right from project conception, IBM took an intelligent approach to the personal computer field. It noticed that the market for personal computers was spreading rapidly among both businesses and individuals. To move more rapidly than usual, IBM recruited a team of 12 engineers to build a prototype computer. Once the project was approved, IBM picked another small team of engineers to work on the project at its Boca Raton, Fla., laboratories. Philip Estridge, manager of the project, owned an Apple II and appreciated its open architecture, which allowed for the easy development of add-on products. IBM contracted with other companies to produce components for their computer and to base it on an open architecture that could be built with commercially available materials. With this plan, IBM would be able to avoid corporate bottlenecks and bring its computer to market in a year, more rapidly than competitors. Intel Corporation's 16-bit 8088 microprocessor was selected as the central processing unit (CPU) for the computer, and for software IBM turned to Microsoft Corporation. Until then the small software company had concentrated mostly on computer languages, but Bill Gates and Paul Allen found it impossible to turn down this opportunity. They purchased a small operating system from another company and turned it into PC-DOS (or MS-DOS, or sometimes just DOS, for disk operating system), which quickly became the standard operating system for the IBM Personal Computer. IBM had first approached Digital Research to inquire about its CP/M operating system, but Digital's executives balked at signing IBM's nondisclosure agreement. Later IBM also offered a version of CP/M but priced it higher than DOS, sealing the fate of the operating system. In reality, DOS resembled

CP/M in both function and appearance, and users of CP/M found it easy to convert to the new IBM machines.

IBM had the benefit of its own experience to know that software was needed to make a computer useful. In preparation for the release of its computer, IBM contracted with several software companies to develop important applications. From day one it made available a word processor, a spreadsheet program, and a series of business programs. Personal computers were just starting to gain acceptance in businesses, and in this market IBM had a built-in advantage, as expressed in the adage "Nobody was ever fired for buying from IBM."

IBM named its product the IBM Personal Computer, which quickly was shortened to the IBM PC. It was an immediate success, selling more than 500,000 units in its first two years. More powerful than other desktop computers at the time, it came with 16 kilobytes of memory (expandable to 256 kilobytes), one or two floppy disk drives, and an optional colour monitor. The giant company also took an unlikely but wise marketing approach by selling the IBM PC through computer dealers and in department stores, something it had never done before.

IBM's entry into personal computers broadened the market and energized the industry. Software developers, aware of Big Blue's immense resources and anticipating that the PC would be successful, set out to write programs for the computer. Even competitors benefited from the attention that IBM brought to the field; and when they realized that they could build machines compatible with the IBM PC, the industry rapidly changed.

PC CLONES

In 1982 a well-funded start-up firm called Compaq Computer Corporation came out with a portable

IBM introduced the first personal computer, the PC, in 1981. This model, the XT (eXtended Technology) was the successor to the PC. SSPL via Getty Images

computer that was compatible with the IBM PC. These first portables resembled sewing machines when they were closed and weighed about 28 pounds (approximately 13 kg)—at the time a true lightweight. Compatibility with the IBM PC meant that any software or peripherals, such as printers, developed for use with the IBM PC would also work on the Compaq portable. The machine caught IBM by surprise and was an immediate success. Compaq was not only successful but showed other firms how to compete with IBM. Quickly thereafter many computer firms began offering "PC clones." IBM's decision to use off-the-shelf parts, which once seemed brilliant, had altered the company's ability to control the computer industry as it always had with previous generations of technology.

The change also hurt Apple, which found itself isolated as the only company not sharing in the standard PC design. Apple's Macintosh was successful, but it could never hope to attract the customer base of all the companies building IBM PC compatibles. Eventually software companies began to favour the PC makers with more of their development efforts, and Apple's market share began to drop. Apple cofounder Stephen Wozniak left in February 1985 to become a teacher, and Apple cofounder Steven Jobs was ousted in a power struggle in September 1985. During the ensuing turmoil, Apple held on to its loyal customer base, thanks to its innovative user interface and overall ease of use, but its market share continued to erode as lower-costing PCs began to catch up with, and even pass, Apple's technological lead.

MICROSOFT'S WINDOWS OPERATING SYSTEM

In 1985 Microsoft came out with its Windows operating system, which gave PC compatibles some of the same capabilities as the Macintosh. Year after year, Microsoft refined and improved Windows so that Apple, which failed to come up with a significant new advantage, lost its edge. IBM tried to establish yet another operating system, OS/2, but lost the battle to Gates's company. In fact, Microsoft also had established itself as the leading provider of application software for the Macintosh. Thus Microsoft dominated not only the operating system and application software business for PC-compatibles but also the application software business for the only non-standard system with any sizable share of the desktop computer market.

WORKSTATION COMPUTERS

While the personal computer market grew and matured, a variation on its theme grew out of university labs and began to threaten the minicomputers for their market. The new machines were called workstations. They looked like personal computers, and they sat on a single desktop and were used by a single individual just like personal computers, but they were distinguished by being more powerful and expensive, by having more complex architectures that spread the computational load over more than one CPU chip, by usually running the UNIX operating system, and by being targeted to scientists and engineers, software and chip designers, graphic artists, moviemakers, and others needing high performance. Workstations existed in a narrow niche between the cheapest minicomputers and the most powerful personal computers, and each year they had to become more powerful, pushing at the mini-computers even as they were pushed at by the high-end personal computers.

The most successful of the workstation manufacturers were Sun Microsystems, Inc., started by people involved in enhancing the UNIX operating system, and, for a time, Silicon Graphics, Inc., which marketed machines for video and audio editing.

The microcomputer market now included personal computers, software, peripheral devices, and workstations. Within two decades this market had surpassed the market for mainframes and minicomputers in sales and every other measure. As if to underscore such growth, in 1996 Silicon Graphics, a workstation manufacturer, bought the star of the supercomputer manufacturers, Cray Research, and began to develop supercomputers as a sideline. Moreover, Compaq Computer Corporation — which had parlayed its success with portable PCs into a perennial position during the 1990s as the leading seller of microcomputers — bought the reigning king of the minicomputer manufacturers, Digital Equipment Corporation (DEC). Compaq announced that it intended to fold DEC technology into its own expanding product line and that the DEC brand name would be gradually phased out. Microcomputers were not only outselling mainframes and minis, they were blotting them out.

CHAPTER 5

ONE INTERCONNECTED WORLD

O ne can look at the development of the electronic computer as occurring in waves. The first large wave was the mainframe era, when many people had to share single machines. This was the age of Big Iron. The mini-computer era can be seen as a mere eddy in this large wave, a development that allowed a favoured few to have greater contact with the big machines. Overall, the age of main-frames could be characterized by the expression "Many persons, one computer."

The second wave of computing history was the personal computer revolution, which was made possible by the invention of the microprocessor. The impact of personal computers has been far greater than that of mainframes and minicomputers: their processing power has overtaken that of the minicomputers, and networks of personal computers working together to solve problems can be the equal of the fastest supercomputers. The era of the personal computer can be described as the age of "One person, one computer."

Since the introduction of the first personal computer, or PC, the semiconductor business has grown enormously. The greatest growth has occurred in the manufacture of special-purpose processors, controllers, and digital signal processors. These computer chips are increasingly being included, or embedded, in a vast array of consumer devices, including pagers, mobile telephones, music players, auto-mobiles, televisions, digital cameras, kitchen appliances, video games, and toys. While the Intel Corporation may be safely said to dominate the worldwide microprocessor business, it has been outpaced in this rapidly growing industry by companies such as Motorola, Inc.; Hitachi, Ltd.; Texas Instruments Incorporated; NEC Corporation; and Lucent Technologies, Inc.

The ability of microprocessors to handle multiple tasks in parallel has inspired new ways of programming. For example, in a method called distributed computing, programmers have developed software to divide computational tasks into subtasks that a program can assign to separate processors in order to achieve greater efficiency and speed. In distributed computing applications such as airline reservation systems and automated teller machines, data pass through networks connected all over the world. In effect, a distributed network of PCs becomes a supercomputer. Many applications, such as research into protein folding, have been done on distributed networks, and some of these applications have involved calculations that would be too demanding for any single computer in existence.

Considerable work has been done in extending the reach of embedded microprocessors to the point where these chips will be found everywhere and will meet human needs wherever people go. Some researchers call this trend ubiquitous computing or pervasive computing. Ubiquitous computing would extend the increasingly networked world and the powerful capabilities of distributed computing. With more powerful computers, all connected all the time, thinking machines would be involved in every facet of human life, albeit invisibly. Computers would disappear, or rather become a transparent part of the physical environment, thus bringing about a third wave of computing history, the era of "One person, many computers."

HANDHELD DEVICES

Nowhere has the trend of "One person, many computers" been more visible than in the rise of handheld digital devices. The origins of handheld devices go back to the 1960s, when Alan Kay, a researcher at Xerox's Palo Alto Research Center (PARC), promoted the vision of a small, powerful notebook-style computer that he called the Dynabook. Kay never actually built a Dynabook (the technology had yet to be invented), but his vision helped to catalyze the research that would eventually make his dream feasible.

It happened by small steps. The popularity of the personal computer and the ongoing miniaturization of the semiconductor circuitry and other devices first led to the development of somewhat smaller, portable—or, as they were sometimes called, luggable—computer systems. The first of these, the Osborne 1, designed by Lee Felsenstein, an electronics engineer active in the Homebrew Computer Club in San Francisco, was sold in 1981. Soon most PC manufacturers had portable models. At first these portables looked like sewing machines and weighed in excess of 20 pounds (9 kg). Gradually they became smaller (laptop-, notebook-, and then sub-notebook-size) and came with more powerful processors. These devices allowed people to use computers not only in the office or at home but also while traveling—on airplanes, in waiting rooms, or even at the beach.

PDAs

As the size of computers continued to shrink and microprocessors became more and more powerful, researchers and entrepreneurs explored new possibilities in mobile computing. In the late 1980s and early '90s, several companies came out with handheld computers, called personal digital assistants (PDAs). PDAs typically replaced the cathode-ray-tube screen with a more compact liquid crystal display, and they either had a miniature keyboard or replaced the keyboard with a stylus and handwriting-recognition software that allowed the user to write directly on the screen. Like the first personal computers, PDAs were built without a clear idea of what people would do with them. In fact, people did not do much at all with the early models. To some extent, the early PDAs, made by Go Corporation and Apple, were technologically premature; with their unreliable handwriting recognition, they offered little advantage over paper-and-pencil planning books.

The potential of this new kind of device was realized in 1996 when Palm Computing, Inc., released the Palm Pilot, which was about the size of a deck of playing cards and sold for about $400 — approximately the same price as the MITS Altair, the first personal computer sold as a kit in 1974. The Pilot did not try to replace the computer but made it possible to organize and carry information with an electronic calendar, telephone number and address list, memo pad, and expense-tracking software and to synchronize that data with a PC. The device included an electronic cradle to connect to a PC and pass information back and forth. It also featured a data-entry system called "graffiti," which involved writing with a stylus using a slightly altered alphabet that the device recognized. Its success encouraged numerous software companies to develop applications for it.

In 1998 this market heated up further with the entry of several established consumer electronics firms using Microsoft's Windows CE operating system (a stripped-down version of the Windows system) to sell handheld

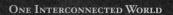

Women use BlackBerry mobile phones at a market in Jakarta, Indonesia, in 2010. Adek Berry/AFP/Getty Images

computer devices and wireless telephones that could connect to PCs. These small devices also often possessed a
communications component and benefited from the sud-
den popularization of the Internet and the World Wide
Web. In particular, the BlackBerry PDA, introduced by
the Canadian company Research in Motion (RIM) in
2002, established itself as a favourite in the corporate
world because of features that allowed employees to make
secure connections with their company's databases.

PORTABLE MEDIA PLAYERS

Meanwhile Steve Jobs, recognizing potential in the
nascent personal media player market, commissioned
Apple engineer Jon Rubinstein to create a product in
keeping with Apple's minimalist, user-friendly style. Tied
to Apple's iTunes media management software and originally touting the ability to put 1,000 songs in a consumer's
pocket, the iPod was introduced for the Macintosh platform in 2001. A version for Windows was released in
2002, and in 2003 Apple opened an online music store,
iTunes Store, a massive media library that allowed iPod
users legally to purchase music over the Internet for
transfer to their iPods. Full-length television programs
and motion pictures later became available for download
through iTunes as well.

The small, sleekly designed iPod, coupled with its
online store, almost immediately became one of the most
successful and revolutionary products of the 2000s. Even
its small white earbud headphones became an icon, serv-
ing as a distinctive trademark of the product in Apple's
pervasive and award-winning advertising campaigns. The
market for iPods and iPod-like devices was second only to
cell phones among handheld electronic devices, and Apple
was on its way to becoming one of the leading retailers of

music in the United States. In early 2010, iTunes Store sold its 10 billionth song.

Later releases in the iPod product line featured greater storage capacity, smaller sizes, more colours for the case, game and video playback capability, accelerometer input, and touchscreen interfaces. From the small, inexpensive iPod Shuffle to the larger storage capabilities of the iPod Touch, Apple diversified its product line to appeal to different consumers. Thousands of third-party accessories, specifically tied to the device, enabled users to further integrate the product into their daily rituals: users could plug their iPods into various products to play music on a home or car stereo system, track exercise statistics, or record audio.

The iPod's name also was used to describe a related social and technical phenomenon, the podcast. Podcasts are voice or music recordings, either professional or amateur, that resemble radio shows. Once uploaded to the Internet, they are available for consumers to listen to on a computer or an MP3 digital music player. While podcasting initially was a grass-roots movement attracting would-be radio personalities, the technology was soon embraced by radio broadcasters and the news media as another way to reach their audiences.

Apple's dominance of the digital music player market thus seemed assured, but that did not prevent competitors from staking out much smaller market shares with alternative players. Microsoft's Zune media player and online music store, the Zune Marketplace, introduced in 2006, were seen as the only competitors trying to add new features at the same rate as Apple. The Zune had Wi-Fi capabilities that allowed a user to listen to songs streamed from its online site, purchase songs and download them, or even share favourite songs, playlists, or pictures with others nearby who also had Zune players. The Zune also had a built-in FM radio, and a user could tag a song heard on the radio for later purchase.

SMARTPHONES

While Apple and competitors grew the market for media players, mobile telephones were increasingly becoming "smartphones," acquiring more of the functions of computers, including the ability to send and receive e-mail and text messages and to access the Internet. The first smartphone was actually designed by IBM and sold by BellSouth (formerly part of the AT&T Corporation) as early as 1993. It included a touchscreen interface for accessing its calendar, address book, calculator, and other functions. As the market matured and solid-state computer memory and integrated circuits became less expensive over the following decade, smartphones became more computerlike, and more more-advanced services, such as Internet access, became possible. Advanced services became ubiquitous after the introduction of the so-called third-generation (3G) mobile phone networks in 2001. Before 3G, most mobile phones could send and receive data at a rate sufficient for telephone calls and text messages. Using 3G, communication could take place at bit-rates high enough for sending and receiving photographs, video clips, music files, e-mails, and more.

The first successful smartphone was RIM's BlackBerry. The BlackBerry's roots go back to the RIM 850, a pager created by RIM in 1999. Featuring a tiny keyboard, the device provided wireless e-mail access, allowing users to send and receive messages while on the go. Soon after, RIM released a faster, more powerful device, the RIM 857. The 857 looked more like a PDA and could sync up with personal and business e-mail accounts. Sales of these new devices started off slowly, with only 25,000 users the first year, but those numbers quickly grew. The first true BlackBerry smartphones were released in the early 2000s. Offering cellular phone service, wireless e-mail capability, and Internet access, the devices took the business world by storm. Even their name entered the vernacular, with "BlackBerry thumb" (a repetitive-stress injury from excessive BlackBerry use) becoming part of common speech. Cell-phone providers soon began adding BlackBerry-capable phones to their offerings.

In 2007 Apple once again shook up the market for handheld devices, this time redefining the smartphone with its iPhone. The device was designed to run the Mac OS X operating system, made popular on the company's personal computers, but its most revolutionary element was its touch-sensitive multisensor interface. The touch screen allowed users to manipulate all programs and telephone functions with their fingertips rather than a stylus or physical keys. This interface—perfected, if not invented, by Apple—re-created a tactile, physical experience; for example, the user could shrink photos with a pinching motion or flip through music albums using a flicking motion. The iPhone also featured Internet browsing, music and video playback, a digital camera, visual voice mail, and a tabbed contact list. For its innovative design in the handheld computing market, the iPhone was named invention of the year in 2007 by *Time* magazine.

The iPhone joined several competing products in the smartphone market, and critics and fans alike noted that it offered few truly original features. The main appeal of the product was its incorporation of intuitive software and its simple, appealing interface, as well as the capacity to accommodate new user-selected software. Indeed, the iPhone and the very similar iPod Touch created a new market for third-party applications software, such as games, that could be downloaded from Apple's online App Store. Apple claimed that consumers downloaded more than 100 million applications, or apps, some free and some for purchase, in the first 60 days that they were offered. By January 2010 more than three billion apps had been downloaded from the store.

The market for the smartphone continued to grow, even for Apple's competitors, in spite of and in fact partly because of the introduction of the iPhone. In 2008, RIM released the BlackBerry Storm, a touch-screen smartphone similar to the iPhone. The BlackBerry continued to gain popularity, with new models designed for both ordinary consumers and business users. Google's first smartphone, a model from Taiwan-based cell-phone maker HTC called the G1, used Google's Android free open-source operating system. Like the iPhone, the G1, released in 2008, was controlled by a touch screen, but unlike the iPhone, it had a physical keyboard rather than a virtual keyboard appearing on the screen. The G1 actually broke little new ground and was essentially a competitive phone introduced after the iPhone and BlackBerry. In 2010 Google took its competitors on directly with the Nexus One. Nicknamed the "Google Phone," the Nexus One used a newer version of the Android OS and boasted a vibrant 480 800-pixel screen. It was aesthetically pleasing, and its voice-to-text messaging system signaled a leap in voice-recognition software.

The proliferation of data downloads to smartphones resulted in a three-way race for the most popular smartphone OS, although none dominated the phone market as Microsoft's Windows OS did in the PC market. According to one market researcher, in 2010 the BlackBerry OS was number one among smartphone users in the United States, with a 31-percent market share, followed by the Apple iPhone OS (28 percent) and Google's Android OS (19 percent).

Consumer demand for information on smartphones and other portable devices drove radical changes in cell-phone networks, which became predominantly data networks. Existing 3G cellular networks carried as much computer data as voice traffic, and the new fourth-generation (4G) cellular networks that were being started up in 2010 could handle and download even more data to smartphones and other portable devices at greatly increased speeds—sometimes at speeds comparable to wireless Internet service.

In addition to the demands that portable computing placed on cellular networks, there was also considerable growth in the use of Wi-Fi hotspots, which functioned as short-range wireless links to a broadband Internet connection. Hotspots proliferated in coffee shops, bookstores, hotels, and airports; some offered free connections, others required payment. According to one research firm, by the end of 2010 there were more than 300,000 public hotspot locations worldwide, and during the year people had used them more than two billion times. The firm also projected that by 2012 half of all public hotspot connections would be made by people using handheld devices.

TABLET COMPUTERS

In 2010 Apple once again redefined personal computing when it introduced the iPad, a touch-screen device intermediate in size between a laptop computer and a smartphone with a display that measured 9.7 inches (24.6 cm) diagonally. It was about 0.5 inch (1.2 cm) thin and weighed 1.5 pounds (0.7 kg). The iPad was operated with the same set of finger gestures that were used on the iPhone. The touch screen was capable of displaying high-definition video. The iPad also had such applications as iTunes built in and could run all applications that

The iPad, 2010. Courtesy of Apple.

were available for the iPhone. In partnership with major publishers, Apple developed for the iPad its own e-book application, iBooks, as well as an iBook store accessible through the Internet.

Almost immediately, the iPad threatened sales of established laptop and ultrasmall netbook PCs. By year's end, it was reported to be the fastest-selling new nonphone electronic gadget in history, eclipsing the initial adoption rates for the DVD player and Apple's own iPhone. Yet the iPad was far from the first tablet computer. Earlier devices had offered a touch screen in place of a keyboard, but they had been offered mainly for business users and had never moved into the mainstream. The iPad was a break with that tradition. It was a touch-screen device with a virtual keyboard and high-quality graphics that was aimed directly at consumers. Its lack of a physical keyboard did little to impede sales because it was intended for people who were more likely to consume information than to create it. The iPad more closely resembled an enlarged iPod Touch than a laptop computer, and it connected to the Internet via either Wi-Fi or a combination of Wi-Fi and the cell-phone network.

Competition quickly followed. RIM announced its BlackBerry PlayBook tablet computer, which was aimed mainly at business customers, and dozens of other consumer electronics manufacturers planned to offer tablet-sized devices. In fact, there were concerns that tablet computers might become so popular that they would steal some market share from traditional laptops and newer netbooks. But on March 11, 2011, attention was grabbed back from the BlackBerry PlayBook when Apple started selling its iPad 2, which quickly sold out in many cities around the world.

THE INTERNET

Handheld devices and computers found their link through the Internet. The Internet grew out of funding by the U.S. Advanced Research Projects Agency (ARPA), later renamed the Defense Advanced Research Projects Agency (DARPA), to develop a communication system among government and academic computer-research laboratories. The first network component, ARPANET, became operational in October 1969. With only 15 non-government (university) sites included in ARPANET, the U.S. National Science Foundation decided to fund the construction and initial maintenance cost of a supplementary network, the Computer Science Network (CSNET). Built in 1980, CSNET was made available, on a subscription basis, to a wide array of academic, government, and industry research labs. As the 1980s wore on, further networks were added. In North America there were (among others): BITNET (Because It's Time Network) from IBM, UUCP (UNIX-to-UNIX Copy Protocol) from Bell Telephone, USENET (initially a connection between Duke University in North Carolina and the University of North Carolina and still the home system for the Internet's many newsgroups), NSFNET (a high-speed National Science Foundation network connecting supercomputers), and CDNet (in Canada). In Europe several small academic networks were linked to the growing North American network.

All these various networks were able to communicate with one another because of two shared protocols: the Transmission-Control Protocol (TCP), which split large files into numerous small files, or packets, assigned sequencing and address information to each packet, and reassembled the packets into the original file after arrival at their final destination; and the Internet Protocol (IP), a hierarchical addressing system that controlled the routing of packets (which might take widely divergent paths before being reassembled).

What it took to turn a network of computers into something more was the idea of the hyperlink: computer code inside a document that would cause related documents to be fetched and displayed. The concept of hyperlinking was anticipated from the early to the middle decades of the 20th century—in Belgium by Paul Otlet and in the United States by Ted Nelson, Vannevar Bush, and, to some extent, Douglas Engelbart. Their yearning for some kind of system to link knowledge together, though, did not materialize until 1990, when Tim Berners-Lee of England and others at CERN (European Organization for Nuclear Research) developed a protocol based on hypertext to make information distribution easier. In 1991 this culminated in the creation of the World Wide Web and its system of links among user-created pages.

Finally, in 1993 a team of programmers at the U.S. National Center for Supercomputing Applications (NCSA) in Urbana, Ill., which included a 22-year-old graduate student named Marc Andreessen, developed a program called NCSA Mosaic. Mosaic was the first Web browser. Just as Apple and Microsoft had popularized computing by replacing DOS line commands with a graphical user interface on personal computers, Mosaic offered a graphical interface to replace UNIX line commands over the Internet. With the ability to display colourful graphics and a simple point-and-click interface for finding, viewing, and downloading data over the Web, the free Mosaic software made the Internet widely accessible for the first time beyond the scientific branches of academia and the government where it started.

Browser Wars

To commercialize the technology, a spin-off company was founded in 1994 as Mosaic Communications Corp. by Andreessen and James H. Clark, who had previously founded and been chairman of Silicon Graphics, Inc., the manufacturer of computer workstations. Clark and Andreessen planned to make the Web even more popular and to capitalize on it by marketing a commercial-quality Web browser, Web-server software, development tools, and related services. In October 1994 the company made available on its Web site the first version of Navigator, their new browser. By utilizing the shareware distribution model of "try before you buy" (except in education, where the program was free), Navigator was an immediate success: over the following 12 months some eight million copies were downloaded. Because Navigator connected to the company's Web site by default, it became one of the busiest sites on the Web. From an average of approximately 1 million hits per day in February 1995, traffic rose to more than 125 million hits per day by November 1997. The browser was followed by several Web-server applications, including pioneering programs for electronic commerce and security.

The company's rise to prominence triggered a dispute with the University of Illinois, which had trademarked the Mosaic name and designated another company as master licensee for the NCSA Mosaic software. As part of an out-of-court settlement, Mosaic Communications changed its name to Netscape Communications. In January 1995 the company recruited James L. Barksdale, an executive experienced with raising capital for new companies in the telecommunications and overnight-delivery industries, to be its president and chief executive officer. In August 1995 Netscape's initial public stock offering created a sensation in financial circles: in its first day of trading, the 16-month-old company's shares more than doubled, giving it a market capitalization of $2.2 billion. The proceeds helped to fund a series of acquisitions of smaller developers, as well as joint ventures with such prominent technology companies as Oracle Corporation, General Electric Co., and Novell, Inc.

Meanwhile, Netscape continued to extend its line of server applications and to roll out Navigator upgrades, adding features such as e-mail and news. In addition, Netscape added a plug-in interface, allowing other developers to create modules that expanded Navigator's capabilities; this "open-architecture" approach led in particular to a proliferation of plug-ins for digital audio, video, and animation. Netscape was among the first licensees of Sun Microsystems, Inc.'s Java programming language and virtual-machine technology. Sun and Netscape also collaborated to define JavaScript, a separate language designed to help nonprogrammers create dynamic, interactive Web sites.

These rapid-fire advances pushed Netscape to the forefront of the software world. Web developers scrambled to implement its latest innovations; users raced to download each new release of its browser. Leading computer manufacturers and Internet service providers rushed to conclude agreements, allowing them to bundle Navigator with their products. By June 1996 Netscape claimed that more than 38 million people were using Navigator, making it the most popular personal-computer application ever. The Web was growing exponentially, doubling the number of users and the number of sites every few months. Uniform resource locators (URLs) became part of daily life, and the use of e-mail became commonplace. Increasingly business took advantage of the Internet and adopted new forms of buying and selling in "cyberspace."

Moreover, Netscape's innovations were transforming its browser from a simple application into a platform on which other developers could build. Observers began to suggest that the browser could become computing's dominant user interface and development framework. Since this analysis implied a reduction in the distinctiveness and importance of operating systems, Netscape's meteoric ascent was widely seen as a challenge to Microsoft, whose control of DOS and Windows OS had made it the dominant force in personal computing.

In the fall of 1995, Microsoft began an urgent campaign to turn toward the Internet. It started by licensing the browser code that Andreessen and his NCSA associates had written while students, and it feverishly developed Internet Explorer, a browser that gradually caught up with Navigator in features and performance. Microsoft kept Explorer completely free, even for business customers, and moved aggressively to persuade computer makers and ISPs to bundle it instead of Navigator.

Microsoft produced several editions of the browser in rapid succession. IE 1.0 had been released as a simple add-on to the Windows 95 operating system. Soon Microsoft produced IE 2.0 for both Macintosh and Windows 32-bit operating systems. This release featured support for the virtual reality modeling language (VRML), browser "cookies" (data saved by Web sites within the user's browser), and secure socket layering (SSL). In August 1996 IE 3.0, designed for use with Windows 95, added important components such as Internet Mail and News (an e-mail and newsgroup client) and Windows Media Player, a computer graphics program that allowed users to view GIF (graphics interchange format) and JPEG (joint photographic experts group) files; IE 3.0 also supported MIDI (musical instrument digital interface) sound files. IE 4.0, which came out in 1997, was tightly integrated into the company's main operating systems, Windows 95, Windows 98, and Windows NT. This incarnation replaced Internet Mail and News with Outlook Express, a freeware version of Microsoft Office Outlook, the company's commercial e-mail and newsgroup client. Released in September 1998, IE 5.0 expanded Web design capabilities and allowed for further personalization. IE 6.0, released in 2001 and designed to work with the Windows XP operating system, featured more privacy and security options. IE 6.0 was Microsoft's primary Web browser until the 2006 development of IE 7.0, which was compatible with the Windows Vista operating system. IE 8.0, which was released in 2009, added more support for Web 2.0 features.

As a result of the unstoppable rise of IE, Netscape's market share among browser users, previously estimated at over 80 percent, began to decline. In response, Netscape accused Microsoft of unfair business practices and filed a series of complaints with regulatory bodies. Netscape also placed a greater emphasis on sales of server applications and corporate services, and it released a new product, Communicator, which combined the Navigator browser with workgroup-collaboration features designed to appeal to corporate customers. Another initiative was the creation of Netcenter, an information and commerce service built around its heavily trafficked Web site.

In all these areas, however, Netscape faced entrenched competitors. In early 1998 it reported slowing growth and its first quarterly operating loss ever. In an effort to regain market momentum, it declared Navigator and Communicator completely free and even made the programs' source code available to other

Google's Chrome browser shortcut displayed next to Mozilla Firefox's shortcut and Microsoft's Internet Explorer browser shortcut, on a laptop. Alexander Hassenstein/Getty Images

developers for customizing and enhancement. But nothing could stop the company's slide. In 1998 Netscape was purchased by America Online, Inc. (AOL). With increasing competition from Mozilla Firefox, an open-source browser developed from Navigator beginning in 2002, and the continuing market dominance of IE, AOL discontinued support for Navigator in 2008. The browser war shifted from an all-out fight between two commercial enterprises (Netscape and Microsoft) to an ongoing competition between the commercial standard (Microsoft's IE) and free open-source upstarts such as Firefox and Chrome, the latter a product offered by the search-engine giant Google.

LIVING IN CYBERSPACE

Like the Land of Oz, cyberspace was originally the invention of a writer, the science-fiction novelist William Gibson. Gibson's cyberspace, as described in his book *Neuromancer* (1984) and several later novels, was an artificial environment created by computers. Unlike a motion picture, which presents moving images on a flat surface, a cyberspatial environment in Gibson's fictional world conveyed realistic detail in three dimensions and to all five senses. It also allowed for a degree of face-to-face intimacy between people in remote places. In one of Gibson's novels, for instance, a woman "met" a mysterious financier outside a cathedral in Barcelona, Spain, though in fact she was sitting alone in an office in Brussels.

Oz has remained the fictional domain of a wizard and a little girl from Kansas, but cyberspace, since being introduced by Gibson, has leapt off the pages of his novels to become a subject of wide public interest and debate. As both a dream and a reality, it has sparked renewed discussion about the social and economic assumptions underlying electronic communication, as well as the role of technology in modern life. Cyberspace has become a region that significantly affects the structure of economies, the development of communities, and the protection of the rights of free citizens.

The most intriguing aspect of cyberspace, however, may have more to do with the evolving relationship of humankind with its technologies. At the root of Gibson's notion of computer-simulated worlds and electronically assisted experience is the prospect of a meeting of machine and human at a near-organic level. Whether humankind will be content with that level of intimacy, if indeed it ever comes about, remains to be seen.

INTERNET SERVICE PROVIDERS

Originally created as a closed network for researchers, the Internet became in the course of only a few years in the 1990s a new public medium for information. It became the home of virtual shopping malls, bookstores, stockbrokers, newspapers, and entertainment. Schools were "getting connected" to the Internet, and children were learning to do research in novel ways. The combination of the Internet, e-mail, and small and affordable computing and communication devices began to change many aspects of society.

The rapid commercialization of the Internet was the result of several factors. One important factor was the introduction of the PC and the workstation in the early 1980s—a development that in turn was fueled by unprecedented progress in integrated circuit technology and an attendant rapid decline in computer prices. Another factor, which took on increasing importance, was the emergence of local area networks (LANs) to link personal computers. But other forces were at work, too. Following the restructuring of AT&T Corporation in 1984, the U.S. National Science Foundation (NSF) took advantage of various new options for its national-level digital backbone service, known as NSFNET. In 1988 the U.S. Corporation for National Research Initiatives received approval to conduct an experiment linking a commercial e-mail service (MCI Mail) to the Internet. This application was the first Internet connection to a commercial provider that was not also part of the research community. Approval quickly followed to allow other e-mail providers access, and the Internet began its first explosion in traffic.

In 1993 federal legislation allowed the NSF to open the NSFNET backbone to commercial users. Prior to that time, use of the backbone was subject to an "acceptable use" policy, established and administered by NSF, under which commercial use was limited to those applications that served the research community. NSF recognized that commercially supplied network services, now that they were available, would ultimately be far less expensive than continued funding of special-purpose network services.

Also in 1993, the University of Illinois made widely available its Mosaic browser, which ran on most types of computers and, through its "point-and-click" interface, simplified access, retrieval, and display of files through the World Wide Web. In 1994 Netscape Communications was formed to develop the Mosaic browser further and also to develop server software for commercial use. Shortly thereafter, software giant Microsoft developed Internet Explorer and other programs. These new commercial capabilities accelerated the growth of the Internet, which as early as 1988 had already been growing at the rate of 100 percent per year.

The commercialization of the Internet made it ripe for the rise of Internet service providers (ISPs), companies that provided Internet connections and services to individuals and organizations. In addition to providing access to the Internet, ISPs sometimes also provided software packages (such as browsers), e-mail accounts, and a personal Web site or home page. ISPs hosted Web sites for businesses and even built the Web sites themselves. ISPs were all connected to each other through network access points, public network facilities on the Internet backbone.

By the late 1990s there were approximately 10,000 ISPs around the world, more than half located in the United States. However, most of these ISPs provided only local service and relied on access to regional and national ISPs for wider connectivity. Consolidation began at the end of the decade, with many small to medium-sized providers merging or being acquired by larger ISPs. Among these larger providers was America Online, Inc. (AOL), founded in 1991 in Dulles, Va. Originating from a dial-up information service with no Internet connectivity, AOL initially served only users of Apple Computer's Macintosh and Apple II machines, later expanding to include PCs running Microsoft's Windows OS. However, in the 1990s it

launched an Internet division, providing a range of Web services and establishing a strong sense of community among
its users through buddy lists and instant messaging services.
AOL surpassed 10 million subscribers in 1997 and the next
year acquired CompuServe, its top competitor, along with
its 2.6 million members. That year more messages were
exchanged over AOL every day than were delivered by the
U.S. Postal Service. By 2000 AOL had become the leading
provider of Internet services in the world, with more than
25 million subscribers and branches in Australia, Europe,
South America, and Asia. Its Internet services included
e-mail (the service's "You've Got Mail" alert to subscribers
became lodged in pop culture), AOL Instant Messenger
(AIM), video, news, sports, weather, stock quotes, and
MapQuest, an online source of maps and directions.

In 2000 AOL merged with Time Warner, Inc., in a deal
that signaled the coming of age of the "dot-com" industry
of Internet-related businesses. In the event, the merger
quickly proved disappointing to both parties. In 2002
AOL Time Warner reported the largest quarterly loss ever
for a U.S. company—$54.24 billion—following the col-
lapse of the Internet stock market as investors pulled out
of stocks with too much emphasis on Internet content
or services. Furthermore, Internet customers were shifting to broadband service for faster Internet connections,
and as a result AOL watched its base of dial-up service
subscribers decline from nearly 27 million in 2002 to 17.7
million by 2006. In an effort to reposition itself, AOL no
longer sought to be the premier provider of dial-up service
and instead tried to become a free advertising-supported
Internet portal like Yahoo! and Google. AOL offered its
customers two approaches: they could still pay for dial-up
Internet access from AOL, or they could pay for Internet
access from another company and still access many
AOL features for free. In 2009 AOL was spun off as an

independent company. By the end of 2010 its subscriber base had declined to approximately four million.

Meanwhile, many new state-owned ISPs entered the business in large national markets, such as China, India, and Indonesia, and these ISPs eclipsed the subscriber base of any traditional commercial ISP.

SEARCH ENGINES

The World Wide Web is largely unorganized, and the information on its pages is of greatly varying quality, including commercial information, national databases, research reference collections, and collections of personal material. To help users answer queries or find desired information in this vast and disorganized collection, a Web search engine produces a list of "pages"—computer files listed on the Web—that contain the terms in a query. Most search engines allow the user to join terms with *and*, *or*, and *not* to refine queries. They may also search specifically for images, videos, or news articles or for names of Web sites.

Search engines try to identify reliable pages by weighting, or ranking, them according to the number of other pages that refer to them, by identifying "authorities" to which many pages refer, and by identifying "hubs" that refer to many pages. These techniques can work well, but the user must still exercise skill in choosing appropriate combinations of search terms. For instance, a search for *bank* might return hundreds of millions of pages ("hits"), many from commercial banks. A search for *river bank* might still return several million pages, many of which are from banking institutions with *river* in the name. Only further refinements such as *river bank and riparian* would reduce the number of hits to hundreds of thousands of pages, the most prominent of which might actually concern rivers and their banks.

Search engines use crawlers, programs that explore the Web by following hypertext links from page to page, recording everything on a page (known as caching), or parts of a page, together with some proprietary method of labeling content in order to build weighted indexes. Web sites often include their own labels on pages, which typically are seen only by crawlers, in order to improve the match between searches and their sites. Abuses of this voluntary labeling can distort search results if not taken into account when designing a search engine. Similarly, a user should be cognizant of whether a particular search engine auctions keywords, especially if sites that have paid for preferential placement are not indicated separately. Even the most extensive general search engines, such as Yahoo!, Google, and Bing, cannot keep up with the proliferation of Web pages, and each leaves large portions uncovered.

Yahoo!

A global Internet services company based in Sunnyvale, Calif., Yahoo! was founded in 1994 by Jerry Yang and David Filo, graduate students at Stanford University in California. Yahoo! boasts more than 100 million users per month, providing features such as a search engine, an e-mail service, a directory, and a news branch. The service actually began as a simple collection of Yang and Filo's favourite Web sites. It was initially called "Jerry and David's Guide to the World Wide Web," but, as the site grew in popularity, it was renamed Yahoo!, an acronym for "Yet Another Hierarchical Officious Oracle." Incorporated in 1995, Yahoo! acquired various companies such as Rocketmail and ClassicGames.com, which eventually became Yahoo! Mail and Yahoo! Games, respectively. One of the major players in the dot-com frenzy of the late 1990s, Yahoo! managed to survive the collapse of many Internet-based companies in 2001–02, but it sustained heavy economic losses.

Yahoo! has battled Google—the giant of the search engine industry—for many years in an attempt to claim a larger share of the market. However, despite Yahoo!'s release of its Yahoo! Instant Messenger, its buyout of the Internet photo network Flickr, and its inclusion of myriad other features, many of its rivals have endured. In February 2008, Microsoft offered to buy Yahoo! for $44.6 billion, but this proposal was rejected by Yahoo!, and Microsoft then rescinded its offer. However, negotiations between the companies continued, and on July 28, 2009, an agreement was reached in which Yahoo! would use Microsoft's search engine, Bing, for its Web site and would handle premium advertisements for Microsoft's Web site—an arrangement scheduled to last for 10 years.

GOOGLE

In the 1990s Sergey Brin and Larry Page, also graduate students at Stanford, were intrigued with the idea of extracting meaning from the mass of data accumulating on the Internet. They began working from Page's dormitory room to devise a new type of search technology, which they dubbed BackRub. The key was to leverage Web users' own ranking abilities by tracking each Web site's "backing links"—that is, the number of other pages linked to them. Most search engines simply returned a list of Web sites ranked by how often a search phrase appeared on them. Brin and Page incorporated into the search function the number of links each Web site had— i.e., a Web site with thousands of links would logically be more valuable than one with just a few links, and the search engine thus would place the heavily linked site higher on a list of possibilities. Further, a link from a

A computer screen displays the Google eBooks online bookstore, 2010. Justin Sullivan/Getty Images

heavily linked Web site would be a more valuable "vote" than one from a more obscure Web site. Meanwhile, the partners established an idealistic 10-point corporate philosophy that included "Focus on the user and all else will follow," "Fast is better than slow," and "You can make money without doing evil."

In mid-1998 Brin and Page began receiving outside financing. (One of their first investors was Andy Bechtolsheim, a cofounder of Sun Microsystems, Inc.) They ultimately raised about $1 million from investors, family, and friends and set up shop in Menlo Park, Calif., under the name Google, which was derived from a misspelling of Page's original planned name, *googol* (a mathematical term for the number one followed by 100 zeroes).

By mid-1999, when Google received a $25 million round of venture capital funding, it was processing 500,000 queries per day. Activity exploded when Google became the client search engine for one of the Web's most popular sites, Yahoo!, and by 2004 users were "googling" 200 million times a day. By 2008 Google was handling some 65 million searches per hour, and the service had become so ubiquitous that it entered the lexicon as a verb, *to google* being a common expression meaning to search the Internet.

The company's initial public offering (IPO) in 2004 raised $1.66 billion for the company and made Brin and Page instant billionaires, at least on paper, for the shares that they retained in the company. The stock offering also made news because of the unusual way it was handled. Shares were sold in a public auction intended to put the average investor on an equal footing with the professionals of the financial industry. Google was added to Standard and Poor's 500 (S&P 500) stock index in 2006. By 2010 Google's market capitalization made it one of the largest American companies not in the Dow Jones Industrial Average; among technology companies, it ranked alongside giants such as Microsoft Corporation and IBM in market value. About 70 percent of all online search requests are handled by Google, placing it at the heart of most Internet users' experience.

BING

From the time of its release in 2006, Microsoft's first search engine, Live Search, consistently trailed well behind Yahoo! and Google. In 2009 Microsoft hoped to change the dynamics of the search-engine market with the release of Bing, a "decision engine" designed to display more retrieved information in search pages than was typical, thus enabling better-informed decisions concerning what links to follow or even, in some cases, displaying enough information to satisfy the original query. Bing also displayed related searches and the user's previous searches on the left side of the page.

In July 2009 an agreement was reached in which Yahoo! would use Bing to power search on its portal site and would provide the sales force to work with companies that sought to do special campaigns on Bing. The Microsoft-Yahoo! arrangement was scheduled to last for 10 years. In February 2010 the social networking site Facebook—which was drawing some 500 million users and was the second most-visited Web site after Google—made an agreement with Microsoft to present Bing results to users searching the World Wide Web from within Facebook. Despite these efforts, one year after its introduction, Bing's market share had not gained on Google's or Yahoo!'s and was roughly the same as it had been when it was introduced.

SOCIAL NETWORKING

Social networking services have emerged as a significant online phenomenon in the 2000s, when some one-fifth of the world's population are connected to the Internet. Eschewing the anonymity that can seem typical of the online experience, millions of users have flocked to social networking Web sites such as MySpace, Facebook, Bebo, Friendster, and Orkut or have communicated via short message services such as Twitter.

SOCIAL NETWORKING SITES

On social networking sites (SNSs), members create and maintain personal profiles that can be linked to the profiles of other members. The end result is a network of "friends" or "contacts" that share similar interests, business goals, or academic courses. The most basic social networking software allows friends to comment on one another's profiles, send private messages within the network, and traverse the extended web of friends visible in each member's profile. More advanced SNSs enable members to enhance their profiles with audio and video clips, and some have opened their software source code to allow third-party developers to create applications or widgets—small programs that run within the member's profile page. These programs include games, quizzes, photo-manipulation tools, and news tickers. A popular application can draw thousands of members to a given profile, generating demand for the application developer's services and driving up the value of that profile within the community. At its best, a social networking site functions as a hive of creativity, with users and developers feeding on each other's desire to see and be seen. Critics, however, see SNSs as crass popularity contests, in which "power users" pursue the lowest common denominator in a quest to gain the most friends. With hundreds of millions of unique visitors using dozens of SNSs worldwide, it is certainly possible to observe both extremes—often within the same group of "friends."

The earliest online social networks appeared almost as soon as the technology could support them. E-mail and chat programs debuted in the early 1970s, but persistent communities did not surface until the creation of USENET in 1979. USENET allowed users to post and receive messages within subject areas called newsgroups. Initially, there was no standard convention for the naming of newsgroups. This led to confusion as the number of newsgroups grew throughout the 1980s. In 1987 several

USENET developers implemented a change that normalized groups into broad hierarchies such as news, talk, miscellaneous, and alternative (the last was created for newsgroups that dealt with taboo or niche topics, and it remains the most populous category on USENET). USENET and other discussion forums, such as privately hosted bulletin boards, enabled individuals to interact in an online social network, but each was essentially a closed system. With the release of the Mosaic Web browser in 1993, those systems were joined with an easy-to-use graphical interface. The architecture of the World Wide Web made it possible to navigate from one site to another with a click, and faster Internet connections allowed for more multimedia content.

The first companies to create social networks based on Web technology were Classmates.com and SixDegrees.com. Classmates.com, founded in 1995, used an aggressive pop-up advertising campaign to draw Web surfers to its site. It based its social network on the existing connection between members of high school and college graduating classes, armed service branches, and workplaces. SixDegrees.com was the first true SNS. It launched in 1997 with most of the features that would come to characterize a social networking site; members could create profiles for themselves, maintain lists of friends, and contact one another through the site's private messaging system. SixDegrees.com claimed to have attracted more than three million users by 2000, but it failed to translate those numbers into revenue and collapsed with countless other dot-coms when the "bubble" burst that year.

Others were quick to see the potential for such a site, and Friendster launched in 2002 with the initial goal of competing with popular subscription-fee-based dating services such as Match.com. It deviated from this mission fairly early on, and it soon became a meeting place for post-"bubble" Internet tastemakers. The site's servers proved incapable of handling the resulting spike in traffic, however, and members were faced with frequent shutdowns. Members were further alienated when the site actively began to close down so-called "fakesters" or "pretendsters." While many of these were little more than practical jokes (profiles for Jesus Christ or the *Star Wars* character Chewbacca), some, such as universities or cities, were helpful identifiers within a friends list. Once again, there was a void in the social networking Web, and MySpace was quick to fill it.

Whereas Friendster, as part of its mission as a dating site, initially appealed to an older crowd, MySpace actively sought a younger demographic from its inception in 2003. It quickly became a venue for rock bands to connect with fans and to debut new material. Unlike Friendster, MySpace had the infrastructure to support its explosive growth, and members joined by the millions. MySpace was purchased by News Corp. in 2005, and the site's higher profile caused it to draw scrutiny from legal authorities who were concerned about improper interactions between adults and the site's massive population of minors.

The spectre of online predators did little to diminish MySpace's membership (which reached 70 million monthly active users in 2007), but it did open the door for other SNSs to seize some of its momentum. Facebook took the Classmates.com formula and turned it on its head, with a network that was initially open only to students at universities and high schools. Since its 2004 launch by founders Mark Zuckerberg, Dustin Moskovitz, and Chris Hughes at Harvard University, Facebook has served as an academically oriented alternative to MySpace, claiming millions of unique monthly visitors.

Facebook founder and CEO Mark Zuckerberg speaks during a special event announcing a new Facebook e-mail messaging system on Nov. 15, 2010, in San Francisco, Calif. Justin Sullivan/Getty Images

LinkedIn, furthermore, draws millions of professionals to its business-networking site and has become an effective tool for recruiting. While MySpace and Facebook compete for members in North America, Bebo is a popular site in the United Kingdom, Orkut dominates in Brazil and India, Friendster has recaptured some of its former glory among users in Southeast Asia, and China's QQ has grown from an instant messaging service to become a major force in the SNS realm. Perhaps most adventurous is Ning (cofounded by Marc Andreessen, of Netscape fame), which launched the final version of its site in 2007. Ning users create their own social networks from the ground up, using software that require very little programming expertise.

FACEBOOK

In 2004 Mark Zuckerberg, Dustin Moskovitz, and Chris Hughes, all students at Harvard University, moved to Palo Alto, Calif., and, using seed money obtained from venture capitalists, founded what was soon to become the world's largest social networking site. Membership in Facebook was initially limited to Harvard students, but gradually it was expanded to include all college students, high school students, and, eventually, anyone past age 13. By mid-year 2009, Facebook had 250 million users worldwide, and by mid-2010 the number had doubled to 500 million.

Access to Facebook online is free of charge. New users can create profiles, upload photos, join a preexisting network, and start new networks. The site has many components, including the wall, a space on each user's profile page where friends can post messages; Status, which enables users to alert friends to their current location or situation; and news feed, which informs users of changes to a friend's profile.

Facebook added numerous features following its inception. For example, in 2007 it launched Facebook Platform, which enabled users to create new applications that interacted with or enhanced existing Facebook applications. This development tool led to the rapid expansion of social gaming options on the site, with software companies such as Zynga drawing tens of millions of daily users with its electronic management games. Also in 2007, Facebook launched Facebook Beacon, an extension of the site's advertising platform that tracked and reported data from other Web sites, including information about users' activities on those sites.

Although privacy concerns were an issue common to most social networking sites, Facebook Beacon triggered a storm of controversy upon its release. Privacy advocates claimed that Beacon was too intrusive, saying that it continued to track the surfing habits of Facebook users after they had logged off and in some cases had deactivated their Facebook accounts. In December 2009 Facebook shut down Beacon as part of the settlement of a class-action lawsuit that also saw the company pay $9.5 million to fund a nonprofit organization dedicated to online safety. That month, Facebook rolled out a new privacy settings update that allowed users to exercise more "granular" control over what personal information was shared or displayed. However, the labyrinthine nature of the various privacy-control menus discouraged use of the new privacy settings. Responding to renewed criticism, Facebook revised its privacy policy again in May 2010, with a simplified system that consolidated privacy settings onto a single page.

A significant new feature was unveiled in November 2010. Called Project Titan internally and quickly dubbed "the Gmail killer" by the technology press, Facebook's substantially upgraded messaging platform was intended to provide users with a single online communication experience. Titan integrated text messaging, e-mail, and live online chatting into an easily organized, fully archived stream of information.

Upgrades, such as personalized domain names and revenue-generating banner advertisements, are purchased on an à la carte basis, and the network software supports a host of third-party applications. These personal SNSs are then displayed in a browsable master index, much like the friends in a standard SNS profile—in essence, a social networking site for social networking sites.

TWITTER

Since 2007, various aspects of social networking sites such as MySpace and Facebook have been combined with instant messaging technologies to create networks of users who "tweet." The tweets are short messages, and the microblogging service is known as Twitter. A typical Twitter user types a tweet via mobile phone keypad or computer and sends it to Twitter's server, which relays it to a list of other users (known as followers) who have signed up to receive the sender's tweets by either text message to their mobile phones or instant message to their personal computers. In addition, users can elect to track specific topics, creating a dialogue of sorts and pushing the number of followers in a given Twitter feed into the millions.

ShimaaHamdan #jan25# يارب معانا ان شاء الله وهخلص منكم قريب
2 minutes ago via web

RHelmii RT @5orm: ظاهرة فى الصمافرة فى شارع المعهد الدينى - الاسكدرانية من
ساكنين يا جماعة #Alex #Jan25
2 minutes ago via web

arabicfreedom78 RT @fouad_marei: Confirmed: protest in front of
the Ministry of Communications in Smart Village, if you're there,
please join. #egypt #jan25 (via @monasosh)
2 minutes ago via web

Ma7moudSami RT @MostafaMourad: الظة المندسة نازلين بكرة بعد صلاة
http://j.mp الجمعة مظاهرة سلمية بالتعاون مع الأبلاى الخفية.. من يحب يندس معاهم؟
/eJc29J #jan25
2 minutes ago via TweetDeck

i1Tn RT @mkamhawi: تجمعك الآن عند مبنى مصر للسياماء الجياسية Egypt#
#Jan25 #Jan27 #FreeEgypt #Tunisia #SidiBouzid #Cairo #Suez
2 minutes ago via web

Mohamed94Asaad الشروق... اتهام منسق كنابة وصحفى البديل بطب نظام الحكم
#Jan25 #25Jan #tahrir #Egypt #FreeEgypt
2 minutes ago via web

*A laptop computer displays a Twitter feed regarding protests in Cairo, Egypt,
in Jan. 2011. People across Egypt used social media to organize mass protests.*
Peter Macdiarmid/Getty Images

Tweets may be on any subject, ranging from jokes to news
to dinner plans, but they cannot exceed 140 characters.

Twitter was built using Ruby on Rails, a specialized
Web-application framework for the Ruby computer programming language. Its interface allows open adaptation
and integration with other online services. The service was
designed in 2006 by Evan Williams and Christopher Isaac
("Biz") Stone, each of whom worked at Google before
leaving to launch the podcasting venture Odeo. Williams,
who had previously created the popular Web authoring
tool Blogger, began experimenting with one of Odeo's
side projects—a short message service (SMS) then called
Twttr. Seeing a future for the product, Williams bought
out Odeo and started Obvious Corp. to develop it further.

Engineer Jack Dorsey joined the management team, and the completed version of Twitter debuted at the South by Southwest music conference in Austin, Tex., in March 2007. The following month Twitter, Inc., was created as a corporate entity, thanks to an infusion of venture capital.

Twitter's social networking roots were obvious in April 2009, when actor Ashton Kutcher emerged as the victor in a race with Cable News Network to become the first Twitterer to collect more than a million followers. While celebrity "e-watching" remained a significant draw to the service, businesses soon began sending tweets about promotions and events, and political campaigns discovered the value of Twitter as a communication tool. In the 2008 U.S. presidential election, Barack Obama dominated his opponent, John McCain, in the social media sphere, amassing almost 4 times as many MySpace friends and more than 20 times as many Twitter followers. This development virtually ensured that future candidates would include a social networking presence as part of their media strategies.

Following the earthquake that struck Haiti in January 2010, Twitter reaffirmed its role as a powerful tool for the dissemination of information. Additionally, it became an effective fund-raising platform, when the Red Cross launched a mobile giving campaign that surpassed all expectations. High-profile users tweeted about the drive to help victims of the earthquake, and many of their followers tweeted and re-tweeted the message, helping the Red Cross raise more than $8 million through text messaging within 48 hours of the quake. In 2011, Twitter was credited with helping to spread the word about social change in Egypt, as peaceful protesters forced the nation's long-standing president, Hosni Mubarak, to step down in March.

From its inception Twitter was primarily a free SMS with a social networking element. As such, it lacked the clear revenue stream that one could find on sites that derived income from banner advertising or membership fees. With the number of unique visitors increasing some 1,300 percent in 2009, it was obvious that Twitter was more than a niche curiosity. However, in a year that saw the social networking juggernaut Facebook turn a profit for only the first time, it was not clear whether Twitter could achieve financial independence from its venture capital investors. In April 2010 Twitter announced that it had a plan to generate advertising revenue, which it called Promoted Tweets. Consumers who searched for key words on the service would receive ads from companies that had bought the right to advertise in connection with those words.

CONCLUSION

Computers have now penetrated every aspect of life, from the private world of personal friendships to the public world of global politics. Computers are present in the workplace, at school, at home, and in cell phones, automobiles, and even kitchen appliances. They have become so ubiquitous, and the programs that make them practical have become so easy to use, that in a sense they are almost invisible; they are familiar, everyday devices, far from the huge and foreign machines that figured in pop culture a few generations ago.

The benefits of living and working with computers are apparent to everybody, though perhaps not truly appreciated by those who are unaware of the generations of labour that went into their invention and perfection—a labour whose history forms the subject of this book. Unaware or completely aware, however, everybody who has been touched by computers has been affected by them. They have changed almost every practical aspect of life, often in unpredictable ways; the only thing that can be predicted for the future is that computers will continue to bring change.

GLOSSARY

analog computer A computer that works by translating data from constantly changing physical conditions into corresponding mechanical or electrical quantities.

binary code A code used in digital computers, based on a binary number system in which there are only two possible states, off and on, usually symbolized by 0 and 1.

browser Software that allows a computer user to find and view information on the Internet.

cathode-ray tube A tube that produces images when its phosphorescent surface is struck by electron beams.

central processing unit (CPU) Principal component of a digital computer, composed of a control unit and an arithmetic-logic unit.

compiler A very large computer software program that translates (compiles) source code written in a high-level language into a set of machine-language instructions that can be understood by a digital computer's central processing unit.

computer chip A small wafer of semiconductor material embedded with integrated circuitry. Chips comprise the processing and memory units of the modern digital computer.

computer program An unambiguous, detailed, and ordered sequence of instructions necessary to solving a problem with a computer; software.

crawler A program that explores the Web by following hyperlinks from page to page, recording everything on a page, and labeling content in order to build weighted indexes.

digital computer A computer capable of solving problems by processing information by manipulating combinations of binary digits.

flowchart A graphical representation of a computer operation, indicating the various steps that are taken as the problem moves through the computer.

graphical user interface (GUI) A computer display format that allows the user to do routine tasks by using a mouse to point to pictorial symbols (icons) or lists of menu choices on the screen as opposed to having to type in text commands.

hyperlink The link between two Web documents that allows a user easy access between them.

integrated circuit (IC) Also known as a microchip. The assembly of microscopic electronic components and their interconnections fabricated as a single unit on a wafer of semiconducting material, especially silicon.

mouse A hand-controlled electromechanical device for interacting with a digital computer that has a graphical user interface. The mouse can be moved around on a flat surface to control the movement of a cursor on the computer display screen.

peripheral Also called an input/output device, any of various devices used to enter information into or deliver the processed data. Input devices include the mouse, trackball, joystick, and microphones. Output equipment includes video display terminals, printers, and loudspeakers.

silicon A nonmetallic chemical element in the carbon family used in the making of silicon computer chips.

solid-state device An electronic device in which electricity flows through solid semiconductor crystals, such as silicon, rather than through vacuum tubes.

transistor A semiconductor device that can amplify, control, or generate electrical signals.

vacuum tube A device usually consisting of a sealed glass or metal-ceramic enclosure that is used in electronic circuitry to control a flow of electrons. Until the late 1950s, these tubes were used in virtually every kind of electronic device.

widget A type of Internet-based consumer software, particularly popular on social networking sites, that runs within a member's profile page. Widgets include games, quizzes, photo-manipulation tools, and news tickers.

BIBLIOGRAPHY

Martin Campbell-Kelly and William Aspray, *Computer: A History of the Information Machine* (1996), is a comprehensive history that begins with early computational devices and proceeds through the creation of the first computers. Joel Shurkin, *Engines of the Mind: The Evolution of the Computer from Mainframes to Microprocessors*, updated ed. (1996), is a readable overview of the history of computers with anecdotes and personalities. N. Metropolis, J. Howlett, and Gian-Carlo Rota (eds.), *A History of Computing in the Twentieth Century* (1980), collects essays by participants in the events described, with hard-to-find details on wartime computer work in England, early computer development in Europe and Japan, and ENIAC.

Paul Freiberger and Michael Swaine, *Fire in the Valley: The Making of the Personal Computer*, 2nd ed. (2000), describes the nascent years of the personal computer industry and the growth that took place in Silicon Valley. John Markoff, *What the Dormouse Said: How the Sixties Counterculture Shaped the Personal Computer Industry* (2005), is the only book explicitly to address the role of people such as Stewart Brand in the making of the personal computer. Peter J. Denning and Robert M. Metcalfe, *Beyond Calculation: The Next Fifty Years of Computing* (1997), contains essays by experts on the social, scientific, and economic impact of computers during the coming decades.

Richard L. Wexelblat (ed.), *History of Programming Languages* (1981), presents an academic and anecdotal history of 10 significant early programming languages, including FORTRAN, COBOL, and BASIC. Thomas J. Bergin, Jr., and Richard G. Gibson, Jr. (eds.), *History of Programming Languages II* (1996), gives a mixture of academic research and anecdotal accounts from participants, covering the history of ALGOL, Pascal, and more modern languages through C and Smalltalk.

The question of who, if anybody, invented the first modern computer has its partisans. Herman H. Goldstine, *The Computer from Pascal to Von Neumann* (1972), traces the development of computers from early precursors but focuses on the period of World War II and after and gives special preference to the role of John von Neumann in conceiving the first electronic stored-program computer. Alice R. Burks and Arthur W. Burks, *The First Electronic Computer: The Atanasoff Story* (1988), argues that John V. Atanasoff conceived the first general-purpose electronic computer before the war. Scott McCartney, *ENIAC: The Triumphs and Tragedies of the World's First Computer* (1999), gives credit to John Mauchly and J. Presper Eckert for designing and building the first fully electronic digital computer in the United States during the war. B. Jack Copeland, *Colossus: The Secrets of Bletchley Park's Code-Breaking Computers* (2006), details the important wartime use of the first fully electronic digital computer in Britain. Andrew Hodges, *Alan Turing: The Enigma* (1983, reissued 1992), is a well-written account of Turing's life and his diverse scientific ideas.

Vinton G. Cerf and Robert E. Kahn, "A Protocol for Packet Network Intercommunication," *IEEE Transactions on Communications*, 22(5):637–648 (May 1974), is the paper that first detailed the overall architecture of the Internet and its operation. An early history of the Internet is Janet Abbate, *Inventing the Internet* (1999).

Steven Levy, *Insanely Great: The Life and Times of Macintosh, the Computer That Changed Everything* (1994), is a breezy account of the creation of the Macintosh computer and the development of the graphical user interface. There are many books about Microsoft, including biographies of its founders, such as the critically minded James Wallace and Jim Erickson, *Hard Drive: Bill Gates and the Making of the Microsoft Empire* (1993); and the more even-handed Stephen Manes and Paul Andrews, *Gates: How Microsoft's Mogul Reinvented an Industry and Made Himself the Richest Man in America* (1994). Ken Auletta, *Googled: The End of the World As We Know It* (2009); and David Kirkpatrick, *The Facebook Effect: The Inside Story of the Company That Is Connecting the World* (2010), are well-researched company histories by established writers on technology and media.

INDEX